GUIDED MEDITATION

Guided Meditation to Heal Your Body and Increase Energy

(Highly Effective Techniques for Anxiety and Unlock Chakra Awakening)

Stephen McDaniel

Published by Alex Howard

Stephen McDaniel

All Rights Reserved

Guided Meditation: Guided Meditation to Heal Your Body and Increase Energy (Highly Effective Techniques for Anxiety and Unlock Chakra Awakening)

ISBN 978-1-77485-073-2

All rights reserved. No part of this guide may be reproduced in any form without permission in writing from the publisher except in the case of brief quotations embodied in critical articles or reviews.

Legal & Disclaimer

The information contained in this book is not designed to replace or take the place of any form of medicine or professional medical advice. The information in this book has been provided for educational and entertainment purposes only.

The information contained in this book has been compiled from sources deemed reliable, and it is accurate to the best of the Author's knowledge; however, the Author cannot guarantee its accuracy and validity and cannot be held liable for any errors or omissions. Changes are periodically made to this book. You must consult your doctor or get professional medical advice before using any of the suggested remedies, techniques, or information in this book.

Upon using the information contained in this book, you agree to hold harmless the Author from and against any damages, costs, and expenses, including any legal fees potentially resulting from the application of any of the information provided by this guide. This disclaimer applies to any damages or injury caused by the use and application, whether directly or indirectly, of any advice or information presented, whether for breach of contract, tort, negligence, personal injury, criminal intent, or under any other cause of action.

You agree to accept all risks of using the information presented inside this book. You need to consult a professional medical practitioner in order to ensure you are both able and healthy enough to participate in this program.

Table of Contents

INTRODUCTION 1

CHAPTER 1: UNDERSTANDING GUIDED MEDITATION 3

CHAPTER 2: MEDITATION REDUCES STRESS. 30

CHAPTER 3: APPROACH HEALING WITH AWARENESS 56

CHAPTER 4: DEVELOPING MINDFULNESS-BASED COGNITIVE THERAPY 63

CHAPTER 5: FALL ASLEEP AFFIRMATIONS BEFORE BED MEDITATION | 10 MINUTES | 604 WORDS 71

CHAPTER 6: REMOTE ISLAND 84

CHAPTER 7: GUIDED MEDITATION FOR HAPPINESS 99

CHAPTER 8: GROUP MEDITATION 110

CHAPTER 9: THE ART OF CULTIVATING STILLNESS AND RELAXATION 120

CHAPTER 10: MEDITATION IN THE MIND 133

CHAPTER 11: BRING LIFE AND MEDITATION TOGETHER 153

CHAPTER 12: SELF-HEALING PROCESS 157

CONCLUSION 192

Introduction

This book contains information on the several types of meditation, and the techniques on how to do it. We are going to discuss these types of meditations and apply them one by one with the goal of extracting the desired result for each one.

We shall talk about the reasons why we need to meditate, which in most cases a tool that we can use to counter toxic levels of stress and the inability to relax. This almost always results to tension and the lack of sleep. Otherwise, meditation is actually a mind exercise if you will. It produces a sense of well-being, and it has become so useful in this harried and busy world that we live in, you can use it as defense from mental and even physical pollution.

We aim to provide a step-by-step guide on how you can do your first meditation as a beginner and encourage you to continue once you feel that the benefits are taking effect. On the other hand, if you are an existing practitioner of meditation, we will provide you information on other ways that you can do it, and possibly some things that you might haven't even heard about yet.

Thanks for downloading this book, I hope you enjoy it!

Chapter 1: Understanding Guided Meditation

Nowadays, with many individuals around the globe struggling with insomnia, sleep may be an enigmatic term and impossible to capture and manage. Stress and an underactive mind will always get in the way of bringing us a decent quality sleep, due to our crazy quick planet. Consequently, learning how to settle down and get a good night's sleep every night is important. The study has shown that mindfulness will relax the mind in this respect and help to encourage higher quality sleep.

It is a piece of common knowledge that we all need to release stress and tension from our bodies and minds to be able to fall asleep. However, for novices who have never meditated before, it can be a little intimidating at first. Given the benefits of meditation, many people feel overwhelmed by the prospect of learning how to meditate. This is where guided meditation comes in. It is much easier to get going, as it takes away from the novice a lot of mental legwork. All one has to do is follow along with the instructions.

Therefore, this chapter will elaborate on everything you need to know about guided meditation for sleep. For all the beginners looking for a detailed introduction to guided meditation, this is going to be very enlightening. First, we will shed light on the basics of guided meditation. Then, we'll get into the science behind guided meditation and how it impacts our brainwave patterns. Then, the chapter will focus on how guided meditation differs from unguided or self-guided meditation practices. Finally, the last part of the chapter will entail differences between guided meditation and hypnosis, along with a discussion on each of their strengths and applications.

1.1 What Is Guided Meditation?

Guided meditation is one state of calmed focus that is guided by another. Guided meditation is when you are directed by a narrator to induce calm and elicit a specific difference in your life. First, you are guided to relax your mind and body, to help you move into a deeper meditative state before you embark on a path, in your mind, to reach a particular objective. It can be a yoga instructor, a religious guide, a CD, or even a playback video of you to yourself. The tutorial will advise you to relax the various muscles in your body until they're calm. Then, he/she will lead you through a sequence of mental pictures and soothing light visualizations or the dissipation of any past errors. Guided meditation on the sleep can be as short as a few minutes, or as long as a few hours. In either case, the goal is to achieve spiritual, physical, and emotional healing and stress relief. Even though the mind has a propensity to wander everywhere it can, all of us find it harder to focus and relax when our brains are not left completely to their own devices; a real-life guide guides this kind of meditation. Here, by combining usual thinking with soothing pictures and sounds that are conducive to a state of ease, you begin to let go of anxieties and restlessness.

Not all guided meditations are created equally, but in almost all sessions or recordings, there are similar characteristics. First, the guide will help you relax different muscle groups by deepening your breathing and releasing stress. There may be a moment of grounding, where the guide asks you to imagine your bones and feet forming roots in the ground. You'll be told to listen to your breath or pulse in the present moment carefully. The guide may make you imagine a soothing light that fills the body and dispels any sickness or negative energy. Sometimes, the most intense guided meditations will make you imagine transmitting healing light to those that hurt you in the past. Then, you will be asked to refocus on your breathing by the guide, and have your toes and fingers wiggle to slowly bring you back.

Ideally, your guided meditation will involve calming meditation music that will help you relax even deeper. Some guided meditations often contain sounds of nature that are synchronized with the visualizations by which you are directed during your meditation. For instance, if you are driven to see yourself standing in a forest, you can hear the sounds of birds and trees in the wind. The sound of the waterfall can become apparent as you approach a waterfall.

You will find that when you listen to guided meditation audio productions that provide a vibrant tapestry of visualizations, music, and ambient sounds, your senses will be absorbed in the experience, and you will be drawn deeper into the meditation. This calm and relaxed state of mind and body works excellently to induce sleep.

Simply put, guided meditation on sleep involves meditating before sleep, usually when you lie in bed. Although you can perform your own sleep meditation, guided perform typically involves listening to any audio recording that guides you through the guided sleep meditation. The purpose of guided sleep meditation is to reduce the effect of worrisome thoughts and stress on your sleep and body. You will start to notice changes in your ability to fall and stay asleep by learning how to shift your focus and relax your body.

1.2 How Does Guided Meditation Work?

In order to fully understand how guided meditation works, it is imperative to first understand how the brain waves work throughout the day.

Brain waves are produced when neurons communicate with one another inside your brain. They are electrical signals which are synchronized. Every time you have thoughts, emotions, and behaviors, different types of brain waves are formed. Brain waves vary according to your mood and behavior. When you have thoughts, emotions, and actions, various types of brain waves are generated. Depending on the mood and behavior, the brain waves vary. There are five types of brainwaves.

Gamma waves are related to intense concentration. Gamma waves minimize fear and anxiety and increase positive emotions. They increased symptoms and depressed feelings. These brain waves occur at frequencies ranging from about 30 to 100Hz. That is a state of hyperactivity and active learning in the brain. Gamma state is the most suitable time for the retention of information. That is why self-help gurus and other educators have audiences jumping up and down or dancing around–raising the possibility of positive knowledge assimilation and meaningful improvement in one's state. However, if it is over-stimulated, it may lead to anxiety.

Beta waves occur at a frequency of 13-32 Hz. As the brain works on goal-activities such as organizing an event or pondering about a problem, they become involved. Beta waves build awareness and concentration improvement. They through logical thinking and improve the capacity for conversation. For most of the day, that's where we work. Beta is correlated with the prefrontal cortex alert mind-state. This is a "working" or thinking mind state, which includes analyzing, planning, evaluation, and categorization.

Alpha waves are known to be the most common brain waves that occur at the start of meditation as you attempt to go deeper into your mind. They're electromagnetic oscillations with an 8-13 Hz frequency spectrum. The nervous system is calmed by alpha waves: we lower heart rate and blood pressure. The waves reduce stress hormone production and encourage relaxation. This is the state in which brain waves begin to slow our thinking mind. We are calmer, quieter, and more grounded. After a rigorous yoga lesson, a walk through the woods, a pleasurable sexual experience, or during any activity that helps calm the body and mind, we always find ourselves in an alpha state. We are lucid, reflective, at ease, and with a slightly diffused awareness. It is also followed by a glow from inside and/or out. The brain hemispheres are more balanced. Theta waves range from 4-8 Hz, where we start meditating. This is the stage where the verbal / thinking mind transforms into the meditative/visual mind. We start moving from the planning mind to a deeper state of awareness (often perceived as drowsy), with better intuition, the greater potential for wholeness, and complicated problem-solving. The Theta state is correlated with the sixth chakra (third eye), and we can practice visualization in this state. Theta waves are also associated with the "third eye" because, according to spiritual beliefs, they help us tap into our wisdom. Those become prevalent when we do some automatic activity such as driving, washing clothes, hair shampoos, folding clothing, etc. They're also involved in supernatural and daydreaming phenomena. Theta waves provide a productive state of mind and stimulate creativity. They improve your ability to solve problems and increase your memory. The waves are enhancing your concentration and keeping you still and balanced.

Delta waves state is the final state, where brain waves range from 1 to 3 Hz. This can be accomplished in an alert, awakened phase only by Tibetan monks who have been meditating for decades. But, most of us enter this final state during deep, dreamless sleep. Such brainwaves are connected to the deepest stages of sleep. Delta waves make two anti-hormones, DHEA and melatonin, more active. They help cultivate deep compassion and empathy for others, develop social intelligence, and avoid conflict. These waves make healing faster. The brain primarily experiences theta waves during meditation. Such waves are associated with a calm state of mind in contrast with alpha waves associated with an excited state of mind. Slower brain waves make you feel exhausted and sluggish, whereas higher frequency brain waves make you alert and active.

Many of us spend our time in the beta brainwave stage in this fast-paced world. We go at 100 miles per hour, so we are constantly switching on and rising our stress rates, which are detrimental to our bodies, minds, and, ultimately, our sleep. Guided meditation helps you hit the brainwave rhythms of Alpha and Theta which is much more calming and can help us cope with the day--life in a much calmer, more organized, and more concentrated manner. It's also been shown to have physical, mental, emotional, and spiritual benefits for us. Guided meditation helps one to shift and relax the mind from higher frequency brain waves to lower frequency. Slower wavelengths allow more time between thoughts, which then gives us more opportunities to choose the thoughts in which we invest skillfully. Our mind and bodywork in unison and the brain waves begin to calm and slow down as the body starts to relax and fall asleep.

Guided therapy allows one to be less conscious of the current moment, and more mindful of it. The mind's propensity to get lost in contemplation while we sit and remain still suddenly is maybe the strongest at bedtime. Sleep mediation is a simple, directed activity that gives a natural lift to sleep all by itself, allowing us to let go of the day — anything that has happened and all that has been said — so that we can calm our mind while relaxing the body at the same time. Scientifically, meditation improves lower heart rate by sparking the nervous system and promoting slower respiration, thus raising the possibility of a decent quality night's sleep. It is one of the simplest ways to reach a state of deep relaxation and inner calmness, and it is one of the most effective ways of reducing stress and bringing about positive personal changes like better quality, deeper sleep.

Sleep issues are often triggered by stress and anxiety, but meditation helps boost your response to relaxation. It also modifies autonomic nervous system control, which decreases how easily you are awakened. Guided meditation also increases melatonin (sleep hormone), serotonin (melatonin precursor), decreases heart rate, decreases blood pressure, and activates brain parts that control sleep. The body faces similar changes in early sleep stages. As a consequence, by making such improvements, meditation will promote sleep.

You don't need to learn how to meditate with a guided meditation. All that is required is that you listen, and move effortlessly into your subconscious mind's renewing waters. The subconscious mind manages your body's 37.2 trillion cells and also regulates and integrates all 12 systems that keep you alive and healthy, including the cardiovascular (heart), endocrine, respiratory, nervous, immune, circulatory, digestive, lymphatic (detoxifying), muscular, skeletal, reproductive and urinary systems. That's very impressive and ought never to be taken for granted.

Guided meditation allows you to move to be in the present moment outside of your mind. When you're laying your head on the pillow at night, thoughts you've been ignoring throughout the day are likely to start spinning in your mind all of a sudden. It can be difficult to manage erratic thoughts without any outside stimuli, which can lead to anxiety and depression.

Guided meditation on sleep allows you to let go of the spinning emotions, and relax your mind. This, in effect, stimulates your parasympathetic nervous system, helping to reduce your heart rate and slow down your breathing rate. All these changes prepare you for sleep— in the middle of the meditation session, you may even find yourself going off to sleep. Note that controlled sleep meditation isn't about forcing yourself to sleep. Sleep will be a side effect of the practice, to relax your body and calm your mind.

1.3 Guided Vs. Self-Guided Meditation

When newcomers start their before-bed meditation routine for better sleep, they get confused about whether to use guided or self-guided meditation. Both of them have their own benefits. Guided meditation might suit some people, while others might do very well with self-guided meditation. Whatever they choose, it has the same benefits when it comes to having a restful night's sleep.

Controlled meditation is simply listening to a teacher who guides you through a meditation cycle. They're giving instructions, and you're just following their instructions. Normally, a teacher instructs you to sit down quietly, relax, breathe, and then meditate.

Guided meditation can be a life-saver, when you first begin to meditate, when you are especially nervous or stressed out, or when you decide to practice a new technique of meditation. The potential downside to guided meditation is that any time you receive a new instruction from the person who is narrating, you will be taken out of whatever meditative state you were in. It's very helpful for beginners because it helps them create a structured meditation process that they can practice every time. It results in inconsistency and a solid foundation for mindfulness.

The best meditation really is the one you do consistently. The more often you meditate, the more effective it will be. If you find it hard to sit in silence, then you can prefer to use guided meditations to ensure that you sit regularly. Self-guided meditations are also more difficult because you have to do it all yourself, and disturbances such as emotions and thoughts more frequently occur in the silence. This discourages the practice of mindfulness for sleep-deprived.

1.4 Difference Between Guided Meditation and Hypnosis

Many times, when rookie meditators start out their daily practice, they usually come across many hypnosis videos and audios along with guided meditation. And, it is natural to be confused between the two. So let's find out the difference. But, before we get into the difference, it would be great to discuss hypnosis and guided meditation briefly.

Hypnosis

It is a voluntary experience, where the patient reacts to the hypnotist's suggestions. The patient enters a trance-like state using the hypnotist's advice and even by his touch. There are several methods of hypnotizing others, depending on what method the hypnotist has been practicing.

Hypnotherapy, also known as therapeutic hypnotherapy or directed hypnosis, is generally described as a type of therapy in which a therapist directs an individual into a state of deep relaxation. Hypnotherapy takes you in a trance-like environment where the psychiatrist lets you start a dynamic cycle of recalibrating mental patterns and modes of thought, thus gradually achieving harmony and freedom of mind.

Hypnotherapy has been proving successful in promoting the cure of a wide variety of emotional and physical disorders for over a hundred years. These psychological disorders include the following:

Phobias
Sleep Issues
Weight Loss
Depression and anxiety

Pain Control
Addiction
Sexual issues

A clear session of hypnotherapy begins with your psychiatrist, telling you about your issues and the expectations you hope to accomplish at the end of the session. You will need to work closely to come up with a treatment strategy that combines the thoughts and insights that continue to be embedded in the subconscious mind. The hypnotherapist will assist you with a sequence of controlled stimulation and deep focus cycles to reach the hypnotic or trance-like condition.

By this stage, you're too focused on a particular thing or thought you're blocking everything things around you for the moment. This even renders you highly suggestible, so the hypnotherapist should take advantage of this ability and use a cool, assertive voice and formulate the recommendations.

Guided Meditation

It is when you are directed by a narrator through a scene in your mind to act directly on the desired outcome in your life. You are first assisted with a muscle relaxation exercise to calm your whole body. Then, you are guided through a scene in your mind to help change your life in some way. You are going to use your imagination to help change the process. Guided meditation, with the gentle encouragement of a guide, is about using the power of your own imagination to plant the images in your subconscious mind to bring change.

It makes use of your own imagination to help you replace the pictures and movies you play in your mind repeatedly. The guided meditation is a way of replacing these images and films with new and better images and films to bring about the transition. The focus is on you, the person who uses the power of your imagination. Everyone can comfortably do a guided meditation.

Directed meditation is the process by which an individual — or community of individuals — achieve a state of mental calm and equilibrium, directed by a qualified practitioner, in simple terms. Guidance can be issued in several ways. The expert may deliver it in person, in a written document, sound recording, or video, integrating music, verbal guidance, or a combination of both.

Guided meditation has proven effective in enhancing the care of multiple medical conditions. It may be used as a tool to attain the following:

Enhance coping skills

Lower stress rates

Reducing the frequency, severity, and length of asthmatic series

Mitigation of anxiety

Emotional regulation

Reduction of insomnia

Managing and regulating pain

Enhancement of well-being general feeling

Addictions rehabilitation

The directed method of meditation is comparatively straightforward. This includes an individual or a party, being guided by an expert. Participants may prefer to get a specialist in person, or may even choose to utilize certain tools such as audio, video, or written text.

It begins with the guide offering you directions to calm the various muscles in your body when you sit or lay down. After the relaxing cycle, you'll be directed by a sequence of visualizations. When you move further the subconscious becomes simpler and more open to constructive feedback. At this point, the calming sound of your guide takes your mind through an emotional path intended to improve different facets of your life. However, however you plan to do, this is the stage that everything happens. A full guided mediation workshop will last as short as five minutes, or maybe a maximum one hour, depending on your target and plans with your teacher.

The Difference

Secondly, a type of hypnotherapy called empirical hypnotherapy is used to find the root cause of such illnesses. Conversely, directed meditation, particularly when applied to a community, has no analytical purpose. In fact, it's usually one-directional, so several often, the sound of the speaker is the only one in the classroom. And the interaction between teachers and participants is minimal. Hypnotherapy provides a more intimate approach to it because the professional becomes more focused on one individual at a particular time, creating the room for any conversation.

Hypnosis and controlled therapy have several similarities, but the main distinction is that the hypnotist utilizes precise ideas, phrases, and contact to induce a trance-like condition. This causes the individual to experience a type of extreme, hypnotic state and concentrated concentration to allow ideas for the subconscious mind to infiltrate. But to enter the subconscious mind, guided meditation does not require any trance-like condition, but instead a meditative attitude and creativity.

Guided meditation involves the use of structured texts which contain which sets of meditative guidance. This is because the professor is built to represent a wide public. A hypnotherapy session requires limited coding, by contrast. That is how the professional is usually expected to respond to the client's continuously evolving needs.

Hypnotherapy puts a strong focus on the therapist's abilities to trigger hypnotic experiences when adding sensory stimuli and harnessing the influence of social change ideas. On the other side, directed meditation relies mostly on planting visualizations into the subconscious portion of the mind to bring in the shift you crave. You have only an instructor's voice to guide you. Furthermore, in situations like self-hypnosis without an external influencer, one should create conceptual visualizations.

One can say that guided meditation is a part of hypnosis. In guided meditation, you are encouraged to relax and bring attention to your inner experience. You allow the widening of your perceptions so that you can tap into your conscious and unconscious resources. Psychological theories and a thorough comprehension of psyche and personality guide the hypnotherapy or clinical hypnosis. Hence, hypnosis is incorporated into the framework of counseling or psychotherapy. But, guided meditation is not always a part of counseling.

Defined imagery is visual and sensory-oriented. It is used for a defined purpose (such as health, relaxation, success, and emotional release). You are guided on a visual experience incorporating all of the five senses: smell imagined sight, hearing, touch, taste. The journey you take can be generically created, realizing that most human beings share common struggles and experiences; sorrow, anxiety, uncertainty, frustration, health problems, transitions, sadness or depression, as well as common desires; achieving their goals, living in accordance with their beliefs, loving and being loved, living peacefully in a community.

Individualized guided imagery can be one of the methods selected by the hypnotherapy expert and the client.

Hypnosis is both suggestion-oriented and invitational: the professional uses his / her voice to use specific phrases and words to suggest a positive result, to provide some ideas about how to get to the result, and to use underused or overlooked tools to help his / her client.Guided imaging can be a part of a session of hypnotherapy.

With guided meditation, the aim is to quiet the mind to help build a relaxed and clear space where we can practice to release the discomforts, worries, and frequent interruptions that arise in our minds. We can feel rejuvenated during our meditation practice as we interact with our inner selves, as it helps to relieve stress and anxiety. Hypnosis does all of these things as well, but it has a greater purpose by reprogramming how we perceive, respond, and act.

If anyone is still confused and wants to choose one, here is a general rule of thumb. If you just want to achieve a sense of well-being and contemplate who you are and get to know yourself more deeply, appreciate your quality of life and find it refreshing–meditation is your tool. If you are struggling or trying to crack any old ways of thinking that do not fit you anymore, or you want to introduce some new ways of being, then hypnosis will be the tool you need. With therapeutic purposes, when we use hypnosis, we will reprogram the self-sabotaging, self-abandoning, destructive habits, and thoughts that hinder you from achieving your goals. Hypnosis can be used with almost anything that you need to eliminate or improve.

Of course, guided meditation can be used to help you relax and alleviate the stressors of your life, but the difference is that you are having to practice watching the things that stress you out and then letting them go as you return to your breathing. This method is equally successful, but when you are looking for more immediate results, it takes longer than hypnosis. Many of us are living in a world that is never silent; it is always moving, ebbing and flowing, very energy-dynamic. We click through social media to be "connected" when all we do is damage ourselves with the judgment we see on the screen. We put the television or radio to stop the silence, which makes us feel uncomfortable. As a consequence, every moment of the day, we get stressed out and feel the pressure.

Therefore, it is clear that the difference lies in terms of the outcome. Meditation is a method of quieting the mind, becoming introspective, while hypnosis is used to reprogram the mind. Hypnosis or clinical hypnotherapy has psychological and clinical therapeutic applications and is used in more formal settings as a curative measure for mental illness and behavior modification. And, hypnosis is not something everyone can do at home; it requires a professional, at least for beginners. On the other hand, guided meditation is mostly used in a personal capacity by anyone and everyone. And, when it is used formally, it is usually a part of a hypnotherapy session to induce relaxation.

Chapter 2: Meditation Reduces Stress.

Meditation is a simple approach, if practiced for 10 minutes each day, you can help manage stress, reduce anxiety, improve heart health, and achieve a higher capacity for relaxation.

Although meditation has been practiced for a heap of years, a meditative approach called "relaxation response" was pioneered in the US in the 1970s through Harvard medical doctor Herbert Benson. This approach has gained acceptance with the help of physicians and international physicians as the ability to relieve the signs and symptoms of conditions ranging from cancer to AIDS.

When our bodies are exposed to unexpected stress or threat, we respond with a characteristic "fight or flight" response. "Adrenaline rush" is the result of the secretion of we travel hormones epinephrine (adrenaline) and norepinephrine. They increase blood pressure and pulse rate, rapid breathing and blood flow to muscles.

The relaxation response is an approach designed to elicit the opposite physiological response from the "fight or flight" response - a country of deep rest in which our breathing, pulse rate, blood pressure, and metabolism decreases.

The relaxation response approach consists of a silent repetition of a word, sound, or phrase - perhaps one that is specific to you - meaning sitting quietly with a correct posture and closing eyes for 10 to 20 minutes. It needs to end in a quiet place free from being distracted. Sitting down is favored to avoid falling asleep. Start your muscles with feet and progress to your face. Although your nose breathes in an independent and natural way.

During a meditation session, there should be an intrusion or disregard of concern or ideas for the first-class of its potential by focusing on a sound or word or phrase. It is okay to open your eyes to look at a clock while practicing, but do not set an alarm anymore. When you are finished, continue to sit, close your eyes first and then open your eyes and progressively allow your thoughts to return to reality every day.

The method requires some exercise and can be difficult at first, but over time almost anyone can study to achieve the preferred country of relaxation. In his e-book The Relaxation Response (published in 1975 and republished in 2000), Benson advises working on technology once or twice a day.

If you are worried, irritable and anxious due to stress, try to meditate. Even spending a few minutes in meditation can restore your calm and inner peace.

Anyone can practice meditation. It is easy and inexpensive, and will not require any extraordinary equipment.

And you can practice meditation at any place - whether you are out for a walk or not, ride a bus, wait for a doctor's office or even in the center of a difficult business meeting.

Understanding meditation

Meditation has been practiced for hundreds of years. Initially, meditation was once intended to help the deep perception of the sacred and mysterious powers of life. These days, meditation is used for relaxation and stress reduction.

Meditation is seen as a kind of mind-body supplement medicine. Meditation can produce a deep state of rest and a calm mind.

During meditation, you focus on your interest and remove the trick of jumbled thoughts which can additionally crowd your mind and increase stress. This process may additionally result in stronger physical and emotional well-being.

Benefits of meditation

Meditation can provide you with a feeling of calm, peace and balance that can achieve each of your emotional well-being and your general health.

And when your meditation session ends, these advantages do not stop. Meditation can help you lift more and more lightly through your day and can additionally help you manage the symptoms of positive clinical conditions.

Meditation and emotional well-being

When you meditate, you can additionally overcome the record overload that builds up each day and contribute to your stress.

Emotional benefits of meditation may include:

Gaining a fresh perspective on troubling situations

Build competencies to manage your stress

Raising self-awareness

Focus on the present

Reduce bad feelings

Increased imagination and creativity

Increase patience and tolerance

Meditation and illness

Meditation can also be useful if you have a scientific condition, especially one that can be worsened by stress.

Although a developing body of scientific research supports the health benefits of meditation, some researchers accept the truth that it is no longer practical to draw conclusions about the practical benefits of meditation.

With this in mind, some lookup suggests that meditation can help humans control symptoms of stipend such as:

anxiety
Asthma
Cancer
chronic pain
depression
heart disease
high blood pressure
irritable bowel syndrome
Sleep problem
tension headache

If you have any of these stipends or various health problems, be sure to discuss the pros and cons of using the attention from your health care issuer. In some cases, meditation can worsen the signs and symptoms related to positive mental and physical health conditions.

Meditation is not a substitute for general medical treatment. But it can additionally be useful for your other treatments.

Types of meditation

Meditation is an umbrella approach to being a comfortable nation for a period of time. There are many types of meditation and relaxation techniques that have a meditative component. All share the same objective of achieving inner peace.

Methods of meditation may include:

Meditated. Sometimes called guided imagery or visualization, with this technique of meditation you shape mental images of places or situations that you explore in a relaxed way.

You try to use more and more senses, such as smells, sights, sounds, and textures. You can also proceed in this manner using a guide or teacher.

Mantra meditation. In this type of meditation, you silently repeat thoughts that distract a quiet word, concept, or phrase.

Mindfulness Meditation. Such meditation is based on being completely based on the mind, or a quick recognition and acceptance of living in the present moment.

In Mindfulness Meditation, you develop your conscious awareness. What you experience during the entire meditation, such as the flow of your breath. You can take a look at your thoughts and feelings, but they should be left apart from the decision.

Qi Gong. This practice normally combines meditation, relaxation, physical motion and breathing exercises to restore and maintain balance. QEE gong is part of traditional Chinese medicine.

Tai Chi is a gentle Chinese martial art. In Tai Chi (TIE-CHEE), you do a self-paced collection of postures or movements in a gradual manner, practicing deep breathing.

Transcendental Meditation®. Transcendental meditation is a simple, natural technique. In transcendental meditation, you silently repeat an individually assigned mantra, such as a word, sound, or phrase, in a precise way.

This form of meditation can allow your body to settle into a state of intense relaxation and rest and your idea to achieve a country of inner peace without the desire to use awareness or effort.

Yoga. You create a sequence of postures and managed respiratory workout routines to promote a more flexible physique and calm mind. As you get into a situation in which you need balance and concentration, you are encouraged to do less at the focal point and extra at this time in your busy day.

Elements of meditation

Different types of meditation can additionally involve different aspects to aid meditation. These can vary depending on whose guidance you rely on or who teaches the class. Some of the most frequent elements in meditation include:

Meditated. Focusing your attention is usually one of the most essential elements of meditation.

Focusing is the one that helps to free your mind from the many distractions that cause stress and anxiety. You can focus your attention on things like a unique object, an image, a mantra, or even your breathing.

Relaxation in breathing. This method penetrates deep, evenly respiration, using the diaphragm muscle to enlarge your lungs. The objective is to slow your breath, take as much oxygen as possible, and reduce the overuse of shoulder, neck and chest muscles while breathing so that you can breathe more efficiently.

A quiet setting. If you are a beginner, it can be easy to practice meditation if you are in a quiet place with some distractions, including no television, radio or cell phone. When you become more expert at meditation, you may be able to do it anywhere, mainly in high-stress situations where you get the most out of meditation, such as visitor jams, a worrying task. A long line at the assembly or grocery store.

A comfortable position. You can meditate whether you are sitting or not, getting down, walking, or concentrating in different positions or activities. Just try to be comfortable so that you get the most out of your meditation. Aim to maintain correct posture during meditation.

Open attitude. Discard thoughts Decide to leave your thought.

Ways to meditate daily

Do not give up thinking of focusing on your stress in the "right" way. If you choose, you can participate in unique meditation centers or group training through educated instructors. But you can also exercise carefully on your own.

And you can make meditation as formal or informal as you wish, though it suits your lifestyle and situation. Some humans build meditation in their daily routine. For example, they can begin and end with one hour of meditation per day. But you definitely need a few minutes of the best time for meditation.

Here are some approaches that you can practice meditation on your own, which you choose on each occasion:

Take a deep breath. This approach is top for beginners as respiration is an herbal function.

Focus all your attention on your breath. Focus on breathing and listening and exhale. Breathe deeply and slowly. When your interest wanders, slowly return your attention to your breath.

Scan your body. When this technique is used, focus on particular parts of your body. Be aware of the different types of sensations of your body, whether it is actually pain, tension, heat or relaxation.

Combine body scanning with breathing exercises and visualize breath warmth or rest in different parts of your body.

Repeat a mantra. You can make your own mantra, whether it is religious or secular. Examples of non-secular mantras include the prayer of Jesus in the Christian tradition, the holy name of God in Judaism or the largest mantra in Hinduism, Buddhism, and other Eastern religions.

Walk and meditate. Combining walking with meditation is an environmentally friendly and nutritious way to relax. You can use this method to roam somewhere, such as in a quiet forest, on the footpath of a metropolis, or in a mall.

When you use this method, slow down your taking walk tempo so that you can focus on every movement of your legs or feet. Do not place a focal point on a specific destination. Focus on your legs and feet, repeating motion words in your thoughts such as "lifting," "moving" and "plating" as you move each leg, move your foot forward and keep your foot on the ground.

Be busy praying. Prayer is the best known and most widespread practice of meditation. Most faith traditions prescribe spoken and written prayers.

You can study the use of your own words or the prayers written through others. Check the self-help section of your neighborhood's book space for example. Talk with your rabbi, priest, clergy or various religious heads about possible resources.

Read and reflect. Many records that they get some time from analyzing poems or sacred texts, and some moments to quietly reiterate on their meaning.

You can additionally pay attention to sacred music, spoken words, or any song you find enjoyable or inspiring. You want to write your reflections in a magazine or talk about them with a friend or a non-secular leader.

Focus on your love and gratitude. In such meditation, you focus your interest on a sacred picture or weave feelings of love, compassion, and gratitude into your thoughts. two

We all face the demands of circumstances in our lives, from minor annoyances to additional serious concerns like traffic jams, such as a cherished disease. Whatever the reason, stress fills your body with hormones. Your coronary heart pounds, your breathing speed, and your muscle tension.

This so-called "stress response" is a general response to dangerous situations, revered in our prehistory to help us avoid threats such as animal attacks or floods. Today, we rarely encounter these physical hazards, although challenging situations in each day's life can set off a stress response. We cannot stay away from all sources of stress in our lives, nor will we choose it. But we can improve the healthy approach of answering them.

One method is to apply the "relaxation response", under a method first developed at Harvard Medical School in the nineteen seventies, by a cardiologist Dr. Herbert Benson, Editor of the Harvard Medical

School Special Health Report Stress Management, Approaches to Prevent and Reduce Stress. This is deep relaxation, which can be achieved in many ways. With everyday practice, you cool down well to dip into it when needed.

The following are six resting methods that can help you soak up the rest of the reaction and reduce stress.

1. Meditation of breath. In this simple, effective technique, you take long, slow, deep breaths (also known as abdominal or abdominal breathing). As you breathe, you slowly separate your thoughts from distracting thoughts and sensations. The focal point of breath can be especially beneficial for humans with harmful disorders to assist the focal point on their body in a more effective way. However, this method may not be as lavish even for those who resolve fitness issues with heart failures, such as difficulty breathing or respiratory disease.

2. Body scan. This method mixes the breath focal point with innovative muscle relaxation. After taking a few minutes of

deep breathing, you focus on one part of the body or team of muscle tissue at a time and mentally release any physical anxiety you experience there. A body scan can help boost your consciousness of the mind-body connection. This technique may be less useful to you if you have recently had surgery that affects your physique picture or various difficulties with the physique picture.

3. Guided Imagination. For this technique, you add soothing visuals, places, or experiences to your idea to help you relax and focus. You can search for free applications and on-line recordings of cool scenes - just be sure to imagine that you explore pleasing and which have non-public importance. Guided imagination can also help you to be imaginative and present yourself with high quality, although it can be difficult for those who have intrusive thoughts or challenge it to encapsulate intellectual images.

4. Mindfulness Meditation. This practice forces you to relax, focus on your breathing, and bring your mind's interest

in the present moment without worrying about the past or future. This form of meditation is loved by the increasing popularity in the latest years. Research suggests that it can be beneficial for humans with anxiety, depression, and pain.

5. Yoga, Tai Chi, and Qigong. These three ancient arts combine rhythmic breathing with the flow of postures or the speed of flow. The physical factors of these practices create a mental focus that can help distract you from racing thoughts. They can also beautify your flexibility and balance. But if you are no longer normally active, have fitness problems, or have a painful or disabling condition, the rest of these strategies can be very challenging. Check with your doctor before starting them.

6. Repetition Prayer. For this technique, you silently repeat a brief prayer or phrase from a prayer while training focuses on the breath. This method can be particularly attractive if religion or spirituality is meaningful to you.

Instead of deciding on just one technique, experts support countless samples to see which one works best for you. Try to practice for at least 20 minutes daily, although a few minutes may also help. But the longer and extra times you practice these relaxation techniques, the higher the gain and the more you can reduce stress.

There can be high-quality moods ranging from traditional techniques (sitting in a stressful role and clearing your mind) to stress reduction and relaxation that doesn't necessarily look like meditation (such as your own Brushing teeth) cleaning utensils). In fact, any exercise that you continue and is completely, completely non-judgmental contained in the "now" can be counted as Mindfulness Meditation, and when practiced regularly, Then you can tell about the benefits of mindfulness for your life.

Whether you are new to Mindfulness Meditation or need recommendations to get started or you are a skilled practitioner in the search for new techniques, we have created five strategies for Mindfulness Meditation that you can try. They all provide examples of how it is feasible to use anything around you as a tool to help reduce your thoughts and static stress.

Sound

While many humans agree that a calm environment is essential for a profitable ambient session, you feel that it is more beneficial to focus on sounds in your environment. This may be a metronome clicking or washing laptop on WhatsApp. Whatever, excellent in sound with zero tones and intention. Music can additionally be a beneficial center of meditation in Mindfulness Meditation, with additional benefits such as elevating you in the morning or relaxing you at night.

How music can be therapeutic

sensations

Paying a non-judgmental interest in your inner and outer, focused on physical sensations in your body, such as your itchy fingers or the feeling of your breath, as if it leaves your nostrils - can land you "now."

And can lead to deeper meditation. experience. Although you can practice the sensation-based method from anywhere, a well-known method is bath meditation.

idea

If you are new to meditation, one of the most important obstacles is the mission to clear your mind completely. It is difficult to stop the regular flow of thoughts flowing in and out, and when you sit meditating for the first time, your thoughts may get louder before they become calm. This is why it is regularly first-class to label the ideas that come to your mind as an alternative to interacting with them. Letting them go can be less difficult with this exercise. For example, you can label an idea as "useful" or "not useful" or classify them, such as "judgment or" fear.

To breathe

Being aware of a person's personal breath can lead to deep, pleasurable respiration from your diaphragm, which can promote physical and emotional relaxation, as opposed to short, sharp breaths from your chest that you would notice during an anxious episode. Can experience.

Basics of deep breathing exercise

Taste

When stressed, people often instinctively use their experience of taste as a stress reliever, whether they are mindless or pleasant sweet cravings given through cortisol. But a sense of style can be a healthy, high-quality supplement to mindfulness practice. You can use your style buds to drown in the current seconds of what you are eating, like chocolate meditation. Focusing on taste can be an enjoyable, easy way to detect pique and relaxation, but additionally, a positive way to eat overall. If you are susceptible to overeating, mindfulness can teach you to get pleasure from each bite until you are satisfied without any problems.

A world from Banwell

Since sustainability is the key to building a strong mindfulness practice, it is good to try different methods and discover the methods or strategies that work well for you. Remember that you do not want a fancy setup - let the surrounding sounds, sensations, tastes and your personal thinking and physique help reduce stress and extend relaxation.

1. Meditate

Practicing a few minutes per day can help reduce anxiety. "Research shows that daily meditation can alter the neural pathways of your brain, making you more resilient to stress," says Ph.D. psychologist Robbie Müller Hartmann as a Chicago health and wellness coach.

this is easy. Sit upright with both feet on the floor. Close your eyes

2. Take a deep breath

Take 5 minutes of destruction and focus on your breath. Sit up straight, eyes closed, with one hand on your stomach. Slowly turn your nose in, feel that your stomach is starting to breathe and do your work to the crest of your head. Turn the system upside down as you exhale through your mouth.

Psychiatrist Judith Tutin, Ph.D., says, "Deep breathing counts stress results from slowing the coronary heart charge and lowering blood pressure." He is a certified life coach GA in Rome.

3. Be present

slow down.

"Take 5 minutes and focus on just one conduct with awareness," Tutin says. Note how the wind feels on your face when you are walking and feel your feet hitting the ground. Enjoy the texture and style of every part of the meal.

4. Reach Out

Your social community is one of your satisfactory means of coping with stress.

5. Tune in your body

Mentally scan your body to find out how stress affects every day. Start with your toes and do your work on your body, seeing how your body feels.

"Just be aware of places that you feel tight or loose without attempting to alternate anything," Tutin says. For 1 to 2 minutes, imagine every deep breath flowing in that body part. Repeat this system because when you focus your attention on your body, each part of the body pays interest close to the sensations you feel.

6. Decompress

"Place the ball again between you and the wall. Bend into the ball, and maintain light tension for 15 seconds. Then move the ball to another location, and practice under pressure, "says Kathy Benninger, a nurse practitioner and assistant professor at Ohio State University Wexner Medical Center in Columbus.

7. Out of Laughter

A properly lizard does not just mentally lighten the weight. It reduces cortisol, your body's stress hormone, and increases the genius chemical substances referred to as endorphins, which help your mood. Lighten up with the help of tuning in to your favorite sitcom or video, analyzing comics, or chatting with anyone who makes you smile.

8. Drinking tunes

Research suggests that listening to a soothing track can reduce blood pressure, heart rate, and anxiety. "Make a playlist of songs or nature sounds (the sea, a bubbling bird, a chirping bird), and allow your idea to focus on the unique melodies, instruments or singers in the piece," says Benninger. You can additionally blow off steam using rocking to more upbeat melodies - or sing at the top of your lungs!

9. Go on

You don't have to run to get high of the runner. All types of exercise, such as yoga and walking, can reduce sadness and anxiety through brain projection, supporting good chemical substances and risking your body to practice dealing with stress. You can go for a quick walk around the block, move up and down some stairs, or do some stretching workout routines such as head roll and shoulder shrug.

10. Be thankful

Keeping a gratitude journal or several (through your bed, one in your purse, and one at work) to help you keep in mind all the matters that are right in your life.

"Being grateful for your blessings cancels out terrible thoughts and concerns," says wellness coach Joni Emerling of Greenville, NC.

Use these magazines to get accurate experiences such as a child's smile, a sunny day and perfect health. Do not neglect to celebrate achievements to master a new venture at work or a new hobby.

When you start feeling stressed, spend a few minutes looking at your notes to remind yourself of what definitely matters.

Chapter 3: Approach Healing With Awareness

Be Aware of What You're Not; Rest in What You Are

Instead of asking "Who am I?" or one of its variants, you can contemplate the following penetrating riddles or paradoxes, which inevitably point in the same direction. Again, don't waste your time trying to figure them out with your rational, analytical mind. Instead, let them resonate deeply and elicit an answer from another level of knowing, beyond the mind. As with self-inquiry, the answer doesn't arrive in a neat conceptual package like the way thoughts do; rather, it overtakes you and dawns on you as a profound, life-changing insight or intuition. Throughout your life, you have used your name and the pronoun "I" to refer to yourself, even though you're a completely different person than you were ten, twenty, thirty, or forty years ago. The cells in your body have died and been replaced multiple times, your body bears little resemblance to the body you had when you were five or ten, your thoughts and feelings are totally fresh and new, and your inner narrative is changing constantly. Yet you have an intuitive sense of something that has remained unchanged over the years, to which the word "I" refers. Where is this abiding, unchanging "I"?

Anything you can experience is an object of your awareness. When you say "I see a tree" or "I hear a bird" or "I know a fact," the bird, fact, or tree is an object, and "I" is the subject. For this reason, you can never know or experience the I, because as soon as you think you've grasped it and turned it into an object, it's eluded your grasp. "I" is the ultimate subject of all objects, but can never become an object of experience or knowledge itself. Yet, it can be known in a more direct way that does not pass through the mind and the process of objective knowledge. Who is this I?

Everything you experience is not what you are fundamental. The thoughts, feelings, sensations, memories, beliefs, images, and stories you generally take to be you are merely objects of your attention and can't be what you really are. But when you're aware of what you're not—body, senses, mind—you rest in what you are. What is it?

Unconditional Welcoming of Life As It Unfolds

Because the boundaries between inside and outside have dissolved in the light of awakened awareness, you now recognize that everything you encounter is an expression of what you fundamentally are, your essential true nature, and the source of everything. As a result, you meet each situation with an intimacy and a newly discovered confidence and trust that everything is unfolding as it was meant to, informed by a mysterious order that your mind can't comprehend. Because you no longer need "outside" conditions and people to make you happy, you're free to enjoy life just as it is, without having to impose your agenda upon it. Relinquishing your ongoing argument with reality—your struggle, however subtle and insidious, to manipulate it to live up to your expectations—you find yourself welcoming what arises as you would a close friend, never knowing who may appear but remaining open, curious, and unafraid of what the next moment may bring.

Aligned with the natural flow of people and situations, you move through life with ease and a minimum of effort, instead of constantly forcing yourself against the current in order to get your way. Rather than experiencing life through the narrow, me-centered perspective of the separate self, you view it from the expansive, global perspective of awakened awareness and respond appropriately based not on your own personal wants and needs but on the demands of the situation as a whole. Ultimately, the sense of being a separate doer or chooser drops away, because you realize that life is living itself through you, and this bodily being is just a vehicle or vessel for the deeper, all-encompassing wisdom of awakened awareness. Despite the illusion of control, you've never been in charge of your life anyway, never been steering the ship, and now you can trust in the greater movement of life.

In the past, for example, you may have failed to enjoy the fullness and richness of your life, with all its ups and downs, challenges and gifts, because you were so preoccupied with what was lacking and what you could do to make it better. How can I get people to love me? How can I make myself physically comfortable? How can I be a better person? How can I profit from the situation, stand out, gain attention, get ahead? Nor could you appreciate the people closest to you because you kept finding fault and expecting them to change. Now, with the dawning of awakened awareness, you're open to embracing others as they are and receiving what the moment brings, without judgment or manipulation, as you appreciate its perfect imperfection, the radiant indivisible beingness of what presents itself right now. In this open, unconditional, listening presence, everything and everyone unfolds naturally and gracefully without need for constant doing, tweaking, or improving.

Of course, problems continue to rise as before, but rather than being seen as problematic, they're taken as opportunities to stay home and rest in awakened awareness, rather than wandering off into the impenetrable jungle of judgments and reactivity. For example, someone cuts you off in traffic, and the old impulse might be to flip them the finger and let loose with a string of expletives. Instead, you feel the wave of feeling rising and rest back into your own innate happiness and openness and let the feeling move through as you embrace the situation without reacting. Perhaps you're able to recognize that you might have acted exactly as they did, and their inconsiderateness is just a reflection of your own since we all share the same human impulses and foibles. The old tendencies and reactions may arise briefly but then dissolve in the penetrating light of awakened awareness as you see them for what they are, without indulging or rejecting them.

Chapter 4: Developing Mindfulness-Based Cognitive Therapy

Did you know that mindfulness is actually a behavioral and cognitive therapy as we? This can be used for improving one's anxiety and stress, and it can help you break away from negative thoughts that can cause you to spiral downwards into a depressed state? This is essential for people to learn since it can stop depression before it grabs ahold of you.

This is something that can help you with episodes of both anxiety and depression. This is something that can also help with negative mindsets that with be there.

Even the Strongest can fall back

This is often used for those who suffer from depression, or who have been in a recovered state after being depressed. A big situation can be a stimulus for someone who has been depressed to relapse into this depressive state once again. Now, commonly people think it's just avoiding sadness or eliminating all of this, but it's actually changing your mindset by practicing meditation and other mindfulness.

This can help to rebalance out the neural networks that go forth in a person, allowing them to move away from the automatic negative responses to responding to the situations in a more positive manner. A routine meditation practice can help a person understand what they need to do when they feel overwhelmed by negative emotions. Whenever there is sadness or negative emotions piling up, that can trigger the relapses. You can use this to help push the evil thoughts away, replacing them with something a lot more positive.

It uses mindfulness meditation along with cognitive therapy, and there is some research that supports that, once it's practiced in a correct manner it's quite useful. If you want to practice it consistently, you'll be able to engage your body, mind, and heart to react to patterns of emotions, thoughts, your bodily sensations, and also any reactive behaviors that can contribute to your depressive state. Understanding and acknowledging the internal and external experiences with learning to accept them, and also working to explore the new curiosity of this with compassion, will allow you to access inner wisdom, and allow you to create new patterns and skillful responses.

How cause and Effect pays a part

As Marcus Aurelius said, the thoughts and feelings that we have holding as true are just as right 2000 years ago as they are today. The thoughts, feelings, along with emotions and the like are what shape the reality of our situation. We often don't think about what we are really thinking, and it often can open up a rabbit hole of different questions, and what others think about us as well. Mindfulness-based cognitive therapy is a way to understand the thoughts and feelings, along with creating new feelings that will create a more effective result from this.

Combining the two factors

There are two factors that this type of therapy uses, and they are cognitive therapy, which helps clients grow and get relief from mental illness symptoms through the modification of dysfunctional thought, and there is mindfulness, which is the state of being aware of the thoughts, feelings, or even emotions that you suffer from on the basis that's continual. It also contributes to the acceptance of who you are as if without attaching the values of the judgments of thoughts. Mostly, this can be used for anxiety and so much more.

How it Works

There are a few steps that you need to utilize, and they are as follows:

• Discovering your own personal thoughts and mood patterns

• Using mindfulness to teach yourself how to be present, and also to appreciate the small pleasures you have every single day

• Using mindfulness as well to stop the downward spiral in life, whether it be realizing that you're the cause of everything evil or what, and from there, emerging and not thinking of painful memories as much

• Shifting the gears in your mind with your mindfulness from the present mind state to one that's more balanced, aware, and much less judgmental

• Finally, using mindfulness in order to deal with the painful emotions and the moods you might suffer from, such as anxiety, stress, depression, and the like.

How do you do It?

Well, there are a few different techniques that you can use, and while you can use an eight-week program with others to practice this, you'll be able to do this with a few helpful techniques

The first is the three-minute breathing technique, which is a way for you to become more mindful of breathing and only takes well, three minutes to do. In the first minute, you think on how you're doing and from there focus on the thoughts, feelings, and the sensations that come from the phrases and words. The second minute of this is awareness of your breathing, and the last minute is the expansion of your attention from your body focusing on the breath, to any physical sensations and how it can affect the body as a result.

The body scan is also a popular one, and we went over that in another chapter, but it allows for you to scan the body and understand what you're going through and what the body is doing

Mindfulness stretching is another good one, and it allows you to practice mindfulness. But, running straight into exercises might actually be a way to overexert the body, and it's important that with this you stretch beforehand, since it's a natural movement that's instinctive, it allows for more flexibility and a range of motion, and it increases circulation by bringing more oxygen to muscles, and it feels good. So, what you do is you start to stretch, but become mindful of everything, from balancing to other sensations. You can use pandiculation which is a simple stretch where you put the palms as close to the shoulders, raise the elbows up, and from there, you can start to let out a yawn, and become mindful of this.

Mindfulness in this type of aspect doesn't just have to be stretching or moving the body. It can be practicing being gracious about the little things, being able to mindfully shower, where you pay attention to the body, the temperature of the water, the way that it feels, and smells and scents you might pick up, or even other sensations. If you feel the mind wander, bring it back. The same can go for eating, brushing your teeth, or even just looking in the mirror. This is super simple, but it's an effective way to practice mindfulness in order to picture what you need to do in order to have a more prosperous, happier body, and one that understands is existence.

Essentially, the goal of this is to become aware of the body, to become aware of any issues that might pose a problem in your life. Being able to become more mindful of your body, and how it responds to such will help with whenever you respond to stress. You'll be able to when you're doing small activities, be able to see what you're thinking and these distractive thoughts, and in turn, you'll be able to acknowledge and let these issues come to pass, rather than be the effect of them.

Chapter 5: Fall Asleep Affirmations Before Bed Meditation | 10 Minutes | 604 Words

Hello and welcome to this ten minute meditation for falling asleep affirmations. Take a moment to settle into where you are. Make sure your alarm is set and that you don't have anything else to do today so that you can just drift off into a relaxing sleep. As these affirmations are said to you, let them wash over your body. You don't have to repeat them unless you want to. Just relax into the experience.

At the end of this meditation, I will recommend a gentle breathing exercise that you can repeat on your own. When I stop talking, simply continue doing it on your own until you no longer wish to, or forget to continue.

Let your mind go during this meditation.

Let everything go.

Your day is done, you don't need to hold onto anything anymore.

There is nothing to do right now but rest.

There is nowhere to be but right here.
In your bed, under your sheets, and tucked in safely for rest.
You deserve a wonderful night's sleep.
Allow these words to float over you and into your body.
Breathing in, and out, absorbing these words.
I have wonderful sleep.
My sleep rejuvenates all parts of my body.
I have deep, refreshing sleep every night.
I am grateful for the wonderful sleep I experience every night.
My dreams are soothing and calming.
I look forward to sleep, and I make sure my body is taken care of before bed.
I respect sleep and what sleep offers me.
I respect my body's need for sleep and I love to give my body what it needs.
Every morning when I wake up I feel refreshed, alive, and ready for the day.
Sleep prepares me for an abundance of energy the next day.
I love all things about sleep.
I am so grateful for my ability to sleep.

I am thankful my body feels gently tired, and ready for sleep now.

I am thankful for my wonderful sleep tonight.

I am thankful for how easy it is for me to fall asleep.

I am thankful for how easy it is for me to stay asleep during the night.

All of my concerns, worries, and fears dissipate as I fall asleep.

I am safe when I sleep.

No matter what is going on in life, I make sure my sleep is deep and restful.

I am thankful for my deep sleep.

And just let these words and ideas gently wash over you as you breathe in and out.

Feeling what you resonated with the most fill your entire body.

On your exhalations releasing what you wish to release.

Let your breath move at a tempo that is relaxing for you. See if you can breathe from the bottom of your diaphragm, or your abdomen.

Let your fatigue and relaxation take over your body and gently drift you into sleep.

Feeling the weight of your body against your mattress.
Feeling how safe you feel right now.
How easy it is to drift off into sleep.
Breathing in at a pace comfortable for you.
Breathing out at a pace comfortable for you.
Breathing in... and out...
Letting everything go as you keep breathing off into sleep.
In... and out...
In... and out...
In... and out...
In... and out...
In... and out...
In... and out...
In... and out...
In... and out...
In... and out...
In... and out...
In... and out...
In... and out...
In... and out...
In... and out...
In... and out...
In... and out...

In… and out…
In… and out…
In… and out…
In… and out…
Thank you for listening, goodnight.

Self compassion for a Hard Work Day | 10 Minutes | 591 Words

Hello and welcome to this meditation for Self Compassion for a hard work day. When things get hard, overwhelming, and stressful, many of us can choose to be hard on ourselves for what is happening. Sometimes it can even feel like the challenges that arise are our own fault. Yet, sometimes things happen in life that is beyond anyone's control. In this meditation we will explore self compassion for difficult challenges that arise, and how to give your body some extra love through the challenges.

Before we begin, take a moment to make sure you are comfortable where you are. Close the door to the room you are in if you feel it would give you an extra feeling of safety. If you are sitting down, make sure your back is straight, your hands are resting gently on your lap, and you feel comfortable to remain there for the next ten minutes. If you are lying down, just make sure your body is straight.

Breathe in, and out, at a pace that is comfortable for you.

Let your day go for the duration of this meditation.

Let your thoughts go.

Let your opinions go.

Let your worries go.

Even let your fears go if possible.

Letting everything go that you wish to release during this time.

Letting your breath slow down moment by moment.

Being present with the sensations you feel as you breathe in and out.

Feeling the temperature of your breath.

Feeling your chest and abdomen gently rise and fall with each breath.

Feeling the slight relaxation your body receives on every exhalation.

Feeling the slight rejuvenation your body receives on every inhalation.

What happened today, or recently, that bothered you?

Who was involved?

What do you wish had happened?

Using your imagination, if you could be on your own side, what would you tell the other people, places, or things that were involved that upset you?

How would you replay the situation so that it feels best for you? Would you stand up for yourself? Would you assert boundaries? Would you walk away? What feels best.

Let yourself replay the situation so that it feels right for you.

When you are ready, just release this image, and come back to your body.

If you are comfortable to do so, give your body a big hug with your arms.

Let yourself receive the compassion, understanding, and love that you innately have for yourself.

Breathe in this love for yourself. Let it pour into your body.

Exhaling out any fears or tension you may feel.

Only if you wish to, see if you are open to forgive those who have hurt you in this situation. Everyone is doing their best, whether it seems that way or not. It doesn't mean you forget what happened, you just release it for your own emotional wellbeing. It is an act of self love to forgive others, because you no longer have to carry the weight of anger towards them, only the peace of love towards yourself.

Just taking one deep breath in, and out.

Giving yourself one last squeeze in your hug if you are still hugging yourself.

Opening your eyes if they are closed.

Taking a moment to receive the environment you are in.

Taking a moment to do some light stretching, perhaps wiggling your fingers and toes, bringing awareness back to your body.

Thank you for listening to this meditation today. I hope you have a day full of self compassion, love, and understanding for the wonderful person that you are.

Stress Relief | 10 Minutes | 745 Words

Hello and welcome to this ten minute meditation for stress relief. With a busy schedule, responsibilities, and a common concept to put our own needs second, stress can easily accumulate in the body. This meditation is designed to give you a quick and easy way to release all of your pent up stress and embrace ease.

If possible, please take a moment to put your electronics on to do not disturb for the next ten minutes. Give yourself the time to focus on yourself.

Take some time to settle into where you are- whether it's on a chair, or lying down- and breathe.

Close your eyes.

Starting at your head, imagine all the stressful, coiled, and tense energy melting away. It drips down your body into the Earth beneath you on your exhalation.

Now onto your neck. Breathing into here and letting all tension go with your exhalations.

Now to the very top part of your shoulders, including your collar bone. Breathing into here and letting it all go.

Letting all the tension, stress, anxiety, and heavy emotions go.

Now making your way to your arms, focusing on your shoulders and upper arm area. Breathing into here, and on the exhalations, letting all tension and anxiety just drop away from your body into the Earth beneath you.

Now your elbows, your lower arms, and your hands. Breathing into here, and letting everything melt away, down into the Earth.

Now back up to the top part of your chest, just beneath your collar bone, wrapping around to the armpit area, and circling around to the strong back muscles. Breathing into here, and letting all tension, pain, or worries go on your exhalations. Imagining all the stress melting away into the Earth.

Lowering down to the pecks or breast area and all the muscles here, wrapping around the middle of the ribcage, and to the upper middle back. Breathing in, and letting all stress, heaviness, and dense energy go on the exhalations into the Earth beneath you.

Moving down to the lower rib cage area. Breathing into it. Allowing your awareness to wrap around the sides of the lower rib cage, and around the back. Just feeling any tension melting down from your body into the Earth.

Bringing your awareness to your abdomen area. This includes your abdomen, your waist, and just beneath the middle of your back. Breathing into here, and letting all the stress, anxiety, and tension go on your exhalations.

Now your lower abdomen, breathing into here, letting everything go in your lower abdomen, your hips, and your lower back. Releasing all tension, worry or anxiety down into the Earth beneath you.

Now to your groin area and your buttocks. Breathing into here, and letting all tension, heavy sensations, and unnecessary energy go on the exhalations into the Earth beneath you.

Focusing on your upper legs, keeping your breathing going here, allowing all the tension and stress to leave on the exhalations. Allowing the heavy energy to melt down into the Earth beneath you.

Now bring your awareness to your knees and your lower legs. Breathing into here and letting all the tension, stress, and anxiety go into the Earth beneath you. Feeling it just melt away from your body.

Bringing your awareness to your ankles and your feet. Breathing into here, and letting all the micro tension, stress, and anxiety melt into the Earth on your exhalation.

Now taking a moment to breathe. Enjoying how your body feels.

Bringing your awareness to the entirety of your body, take a deep breath in, and let everything out on a deep, luxurious exhalation.

Breathing into your body, and letting everything go again.

Imagine as though you could breathe into your entire body and have all remaining stress, tension and anxiety melting away into the Earth beneath you.

Now as you inhale, fill all of this empty space that you have created with your relaxation, with loving energy towards yourself. Feel it nourishing your bones, your nerves, your blood, your hormones, your organs, your muscles, your senses, your skin- every single part of your body.

Just breathe for a little while, let all of this energy pour into our body. Feeling it charge your cells.

You can continue this feeling throughout the day by taking tiny moments to release stress on your exhalations and breathing in love for yourself on your inhalations.

Thank you for listening to this meditation today. Have a relaxing rest of your day.

Chapter 6: Remote Island

Relax and make yourself really comfortable. Imagine yourself on a remote island, you have it all to yourself and nobody else lives there. You are completely surrounded by the sea water. The sound of the waves is such a calming sound. You can take anyone along with you to this quiet and remote place, you could take your partner, friend, someone who is no longer here, a pet, even an actor or actress from your favourite film. You may choose to be alone, after all it's your island so you can choose.

It is so peaceful here and you can let go of all your worries and problems. Nobody or anything can hurt you here.

The trees are blowing and you can hear their soft sound all the time calming and soothing you.

You see birds fly over to the island and seagulls frequently come in.

Imagine what you could do here with so much free time. You could read a book or learn a new language or play sports. I want you to imagine what you would do here on this remote island with its gentle breeze and rhythmic sounding waves.

I would say that life on an island teaches us to be patient because they happen at their own pace. You would have to find water and food, what sort of shelter would you create? It's not a 5-star resort!

Would you enjoy the powdery sand and deepening shades of turquoise on this idyllic patch of paradise?

You are miles from anywhere and you don't even have a boat to take you shopping or to see friend or family. What if you got poorly or frightened?

It's everyone's dream to be on a remote island, miles from anywhere. But is it what's it cracked up to be?

We think we have so many problems and we worry constantly about money, relationships, illness and we could suffer with depression or stress. We think by living on an island would take all that away but how would we feel without family or friends to talk and help us. We have church's everywhere, there won't be a church on an island. We have Doctors and hospitals. We have our children and partners here. On the island there would be no shops or hairdressers. No purpose to our life at all except to survive. To eat and drink!

Maybe our problems don't seem so bad now as we have everything that we need right here where we live. The phone to call anyone at any time, computers, cars and vehicles parked outside our homes. We have it really easy when you think of how difficult it would be on that remote island in the sun. A couple of days in the sunshine and bathing and paddling in the blue sea we would soon bore and tire of.

I think trying to live on a deserted island would be almost impossible, could you catch your lunch every day from the sea? could you survive on coconuts? What about monkeys and snakes at night! Sleeping outdoors in a hammock.

NO THANK YOU

You now feel like your anxieties and problems are not so bad and you feel relieved that you have the life you have.

It's not so bad is it?

THE RAIN FOREST

Imagine you are in a rainforest, miles away from home. This will be a truly exceptional experience. You are in this rainforest a tall dense jungle. You start to walk through this rainforest and the first thing that you notice is the humid heat which is so different to anything that you have experienced before.

It occurs to you that as many as 30 million species of plants and animals live in this rainforest. What a thought! You continue to walk and you become aware of the lush and humid stretches of land covered in tall, broadleaf evergreen trees. You become very relaxed as you take it slowly and you have a long day here and you plan to spend one night here also. You are very excited at this. The temperature has reached around 86 degrees Fahrenheit and you are becoming very warm.

You look up and see a canopy of trees. This area is comprised of the tops of the trees and vines, you cannot believe how large this area is. You look further down and you see ferns and flowers and tree trunks, dead leaves are absolutely everywhere. Where ever you tread you can hear the crunch of them under your feet. You like to hear this and it make you smile!

After a while the heat and humidity and lack of wind makes you feel very tired indeed. You look ahead and notice a river, you become excited by this and you walk up to the gentle flowing water and get in it to cool off for a while. You feel whole again and full of energy once more. You spend the day picking up coconuts and eating whatever fruit you recognise. You have also brought a rucksack with you which you carry on your back. In this you have fresh water and food for the day and a few snacks for tonight. You have walked for quite a long distance by now and your anxiety and stress has completely gone whilst you concentrate on this rainforest experience.

You can hear the woodpeckers in the canopy of trees above you and see monkeys and flying squirrels. You can hear the sound of the high-pitched screech of a million bugs!

The day is soon coming to an end and you have to prepare yourself for this evening. You manage to find a nice spot near the river where you construct a very basic and simple construction from tree trunks and canvas that you have in your rucksack. You get yourself together whilst having a snack and some cool fresh water. You sit for a while and watch the river. This river is flowing slowly over boulders and rocks and trees which have fallen in to it. You watch this for a while and find it soothing and relaxing.

You put a blanket in to your little hut and lay down to try and settle for the night. You suddenly become very aware of the crickets and frogs. What an experience and you love it!Squeals and croaking everywhere.

Then quite suddenly a rainstorm comes in, there is nothing quite like going to sleep at night with a tropical rainstorm pouring down huge drops of water on your little hut. After the hot day, the relative cool that accompanies the rain and the sounds of the drops are mesmerising. It is a simple pleasure that cannot be compared, as you pull your thin sheet over you to fend off the damp cool that filters in through the screens of your little hut.

You feel like you are at the end of the world and feel quite isolated even though the animals never stop all night long.

You survived the night!It was noisy and you could hear the water from the river.

You have really loved your time here in the rainforest and you have learned that you can escape from your thoughts and your mind and your worries. You have control over your thoughts. Unlike the rainforest that has no control over itself with its constant growing of trees and animals screeching constantly and the rain which falls all the time over and over again.

BEN NEVIS

Make yourself really comfortable before I begin this guided meditation.

Imagine you are going on a mountain walk, walking on the highest mountain in the British Isles, Ben Nevis. Standing at

1,345 metres above sea level, it is at the western end of the Grampian Mountains in the Lochaber area of the Scottish Highland. Very close to the town of Fort William.

You are wrapped up in all the right clothes and good solid boots. You are feeling very calm and very relaxed. In all its profound beauty this is a chance of a lifetime. You start your walk and know that it is around 4 miles each way, there and back, quite a challenge!

There is a footpath which you can follow and you start to climb very slowly at first until you get used to it. You are amazed how you are able to climb with such ease. The weather is being kind to you at the moment. When you look to the peaks at the top, they are absolutely stunning with soft fluffy snow on them.

The path is relatively easy to follow but you also have your map with you. You keep following the same route until it seems to flatten out a bit and gives you time to catch your breath.

After walking for quite a long time you reach a beautiful lake and it is covered in a thick mountain mist. The path is becoming a little rockier in places so you need to watch your footing. You then have to cross a small waterfall which you found easy. When it's been raining this waterfall will be much heavier.

You are thoroughly enjoying this challenge and calms your racing mind down. Your worries simply do not exist here. They seem a lifetime away.

You are aware of other hikers doing the same journey and path as you. As you climb higher and higher you notice that the weather is closing in on you a little with little white snowflakes starting to fall. How stunning and beautiful they look. You feel quite safe as you can still see other people and you can hear them happily chatting away.

More than anything you want to reach the summit, you feel that if you can manage this then nothing else in your life could ever be or seem as difficult.

You keep climbing using the steps conveniently provided. You notice that after the first initial steepness, the path does even out to a more moderate slog. The path is very well trodden.

The low clouds are all around you now and it is beginning to snow even harder. You feel tired but exhilarated at the same time. What a fantastic job you are doing and you feel like you have really achieved something so special and could never ever imagine yourself doing this. You stop for a while and have a cup of tea from your flask and a couple of sandwiches. They do taste good and the tea warms you up as you are beginning to feel quite cold now. As you get higher and higher you really can feel the chill from the heavy snow and blustery winds which have just started at that point.

You have been climbing for a few hours now and have almost reached the summit of Ben Nevis, it is a product of a long extinct volcano and comprises of a large stony plateau of about 100 acres with a large, solidly built cairn approximately 10 feet high.

Well you made it! You have done it and reached the top of this very tall and dangerous mountain.

The view at the top was worth everything that you suffered on the way up. The legendary peak towers above glistening lochans and deep glacial valleys. You realise that in Scotland you can't get any higher than this!

You feel so proud of yourself for managing this very difficult challenge.

You conquered the mountain, so you can now conquer yourself!

Try and live your life each day as you would climb a mountain. An occasional glance towards the summit keeps the goal in mind, but many beautiful scenes are to be observed from watching new vantage point.

You've learned that everyone wants to live on top of a mountain, but all the happiness and growth occurs whilst climbing it.

THE TREE HOUSE

Relax and allow your mind to calm down and stop unnecessary thoughts.

Image you are walking through a lovely secluded wood, slowly breathing in and out with every breath. You notice all the dead leaves on the ground and you simply love just kicking them out of the way! You realise this is childish, but who cares no one can see you as you laugh to yourself.

You are walking under a canopy of trees where you can see the sun streaming through the treetops.

You see an abundance of flowers and trees and you love being outdoors, so you find this short walk delightful. It is a lovely warm spring day and the trees are just starting to bud and showing the first signs of green. You see rich wild grasses and meadow flowers. As you walk further and further into the wood you discover an old treehouse. You just can't believe your eyes. It looks so fantastic and you wonder how long it has been here and who built it. It still looks very sturdy and strong.

You ponder for a few seconds and wonder whether you should or dare climb up it.

You decide to pluck up courage and give it a go, after all nobody can see you. You gingerly try the first step and it feels quite safe and secure. You try the second and third step and it still feels strong and secure so you continue to climb up to the very top of this lovely old treehouse. When you finally reach the top, the views are fantastic and you can see all over the wood and many shorter trees and bushes. What a sight and you love being so high up too!

You decide to have a good look around the treehouse. There isn't much in it just a floor and a wooden roof. You absolutely love it. It feels like being in a fairy tale. This idyllic room is hidden away in the wood.

You forget about your worries and anxieties. There are no computers here and no television here or phones. It's all about nature.

You sit on the floor of this beautiful treehouse and take in the view. To be so high up in the trees and a long way from the ground too.

You decide to keep very still and quiet so that no wildlife or birds can see or hear you. You see a Red deer run straight underneath you and he doesn't see you at all! Another couple follow him through.

You feel invisible and it fabulous! You feel so privileged to be able to see all these animals so close to you and they don't even know you are there. You see little mice scurrying around. The lovely singing birds keep landing on the branches around you. They are so close that you could almost reach out to them and touch them. You can hear bees buzzing around everywhere.

How lovely it would be to live here all the time. No one to bother you and all our worries gone. It would be such a delightful but simple life.

Just as you decide you had better get down from the treehouse an owl, a white barn owl comes swooping down straight passed you. You find this unbelievable and so unusual to see during the day. It must have seen the mice.

You very slowly come down the steps of the treehouse and you feel so refreshed and relaxed.

What a fantastic experience for you and you certainly didn't expect to see an old abandoned treehouse on your walk through the wood.

You decide to walk back through all the trees and flowers. You come out of the wood feeling quite uplifted and so privileged.

Chapter 7: Guided Meditation For Happiness

In this exercise, I will guide you through a simple meditation that includes breathing exercises to help you relax and focus on your breathing. This exercise includes different strategies that you can use to increase your happiness quotient. I will help you hold onto all positive thoughts and let go of all the negativity within and around you.

I want to welcome you to this mediation that will help you cultivate happiness.

Before I begin, find yourself something comfortable to wear and avoid any tight-fitting clothes.

You can either lie down or sit comfortably. You can sit in a chair or sit on the ground with your legs crossed. Let your hands rest one over the other in a standard meditation pose.

If you feel uncomfortable at any time, you can stop the recording.

Now, you need to close your eyes and listen to the recording.

During this time, you can release yourself from the stress and tensions of the day and from all your responsibilities, for a while at least.

Let your mind be free to explore, to smile and experience happiness.

Concentrate on your breathing and nothing else.

Feel your breaths becoming deep and long.

Take a couple of moments, breathe in and breathe out, allow yourself to let go of the world outside

Start to visualize a path in your mind. The path can be anything that you want it to be, but at the end of it, you need to be able to see a door. This door opens up the path to your inner world. Now, open the door and you can see a ray of bright light. The light is warm, welcoming, and helps you to relax.

You can see the bright inner world of yours and you need to step into this beautiful world.

Relax into all the warmth and harmony existing within.

You are the only one that knows this place and you are the only one with the key to open up this world.

Take a deep breath and shut the door to the outer world.

Give yourself the permission to enter this place and fully immerse yourself into this world of inner peace. It is a world where you feel safe and you can experience happiness here.

Give yourself this time to work on your happiness so that it spreads joy within your body and eventually radiates from you.

It is okay even if your mind wanders. It is perfectly alright even if you realize that your thoughts have gone off tangent.

You are in charge of your thoughts and if you feel like your thoughts are wandering, you can bring awareness back. Listen to the sound of my voice and concentrate on my voice.

Now, take a deep breath.

Start with your feet; feel your toes relax and then feel your feet relax.

Feel your legs relax slowly.

Feel the muscles in your thigh loosen and then the muscles in your abdomen relax.

Gently will them to relax.

Shift your focus towards your chest. Will the muscles around your ribcage to relax, then move onto your back.

You can now feel the muscles in your shoulders relax and all the tension starts to fade away.

Now, allow the muscles in your neck to relax and move towards your head.

Take a deep breath and allow your entire body to relax.

Your breath fills up your lungs with air.

Start to exhale slowly until there is no air in your lungs.

Take a deep breath to fill your lungs with air. Allow your lungs to expand and once they do, breathe out.

Breathe in through your nose for a count of four.

One, two, three and four.

Hold your breath.

Exhale through your mouth for a count of eight.

One, two, three, four, five, six, seven and eight.

Breathe in again. One, two, three and four.

Breathe out. One, two, three, four, five, six, seven, and eight.

Visualize the path that you took to enter your inner world.

Walk on the same path and the same bright light that you saw now surrounds you.

Walk on the path that leads you through an alpine forest.

There are white pine trees that line the path.

The morning sun is shining brightly and is casting soft golden rays of warm sunlight all around you.

Continue to walk on this path and you will find a rock outcrop overlooking a landscape of mountains.

There are hundreds of peaks all around you; some seem closer than the others.

Let your gaze take in the expanse of mountains in front of you and you will feel a feeling of peace wash over you.

Appreciate the beauty of nature that's all around you. Revel in this gift and be thankful for it.

Enjoy the view and give yourself a moment to smile. Smile at the beauty that's present in front of you.

The golden rays of sunlight are illuminating the landscape. The colors are gently mixing with each other all around you and it looks like a beautiful painting.

Smile and become aware of all the flora and fauna around you.

Imagine the sounds of birds chirping happily and smile.

Now, you will notice a large tree near you. The tree is quite old, and its trunk looks large.

Now, visualize this tree in detail. The bark of the tree looks like that of a sweet birch; its leaves smell sweet.

A gentle wind is blowing, and it blows a couple of leaves away from the tree. One such leaf lands in your hand and you smile as the leaf leaves a slight sweet-smelling minty scent.

Smile at this marvel of nature and take a deep breath.

There is something else besides the wonderful aroma. The leaves start to gently rustle and it sounds like a stringed dulcimer.

Light and airy sounds surround you.

Everything sounds melodious and they complement the wonderful landscape around you.

You are now surrounded by the warm golden light and the wonderful sounds.

Listen to the music of nature; you can feel your heart fill up with joy. There is so much beauty around you and it makes you feel happy.

Look around; there is a bush with emerald leaves next to the tree. The leaves have triangular points and the bush is filled with small berries like raspberries.

Go ahead, pick a few berries and eat them. Enjoy the flavors of these berries and savor how wonderful they feel in your mouth.

Start to slowly chew and swallow these delicious berries.

You can feel warmth and energy radiate from your core as these berries slide down your throat and into your stomach.

You can feel the energy rise within you.

This energy spreads from your stomach to your head, arms and legs. This energy is now pulsing through your body.

All your senses feel ecstatic.

You feel a sense of calm and appreciation wash over you as you enjoy this wonderful bounty.

Look at the bush, the old tree, and the landscape around you.

The sun is higher in the sky and the landscape looks more beautiful than ever.

There are more wonderful scents all around you.

Allow yourself to enjoy the richness of nature and let your body soak it all up.

This powerful energy continues to radiate through your body and it is casting a light halo all around you.

You can see a golden aura emanating from your body.

A pure energy makes you smile.

Bask in this wonderful energy. Let it wash over every muscle, bone, and cell of your being. Let your body be infused with nature's wonderful energy.

Stay in this place for a couple of moments and smile some more.

Now that your body is infused with this wonderful energy, it is time for you to return to the outer world.

Your inner world has given you the tools that you need to return to your day feeling energized, refreshed, and happy.

The beautiful landscape looks more golden than ever because of your aura. You feel strong and happy.

Smile more widely and you can feel this energy shine brighter. Let the sense of gratitude and appreciation wash all over you.

Whenever you feel low or dull, you can return to this place.

It is time for you to turn and go, but the sound of nature makes you linger for a while longer.

Take a deep breath and bid adieu to this wonderful place, for now.

Slowly, start to walk back up the path through which you entered. Allow yourself to soak up all the energy that this place emits. Let this energy make you feel alive.

You feel good about yourself and you are looking forward to going back to your world.

As you walk, you will notice the door to the outer world. Slowly open the door, take a deep breath, and step inside.

You are now back in the real world and you are full of happiness and positivity.

Now, breathe in slowly and deeply.

Take a deep breath through your nose and hold it for a count of four.

One, two, three and four.

Now, breathe out through your mouth and hold it to the count of eight.

One, two, three, four, five, six, seven and eight.

Take another deep breath through your nose and exhale through your mouth.

Start to slowly open your eyes and you can feel the energy of the inner world shine brightly in your body.

Take a deep breath, smile and return to your day.

You can follow this exercise whenever you want a burst of happiness. It will help you to appreciate all that is good in your life and let go of your worries.

Chapter 8: Group Meditation

Prior to discussing group meditation, otherwise called shared meditation, we have to ask you: When was simply the last time set aside some effort for yourself? Whenever was the last time you gotten the opportunity to make significant cooperations? Have you thought about what amount of time you spend conversing with others on the web? Today cooperations are characterized by innovation, is certainly not a terrible thing, except if that is the main sort of communication you get, and if that is the situation, ruminating in gatherings can turn into a lifeline.

Why is group meditation extraordinary? Somethings are better when shared, and meditation is one of them. At the point when you have an intense day at work, you message your WhatsApp's companions gathering to educate them concerning it, and now and again you solicit some from those companions to go out, the two choices cause you to feel comprehended in light of the fact that it is ideal to realize somebody thinks about you and that you are upheld.

Mutual meditation has similar standards, to unite a gathering of individuals to cause them to feel better beginning with their own being.

Among the numerous advantages of gathering reflection, we can discuss these 6 ones:

Otherworldly help becomes more grounded: simply like the customary gatherings with your companions, when you join a gathering contemplation, you make collaboration, which means the blend of at least two sections to accomplish an option that could be greater than what just one could do.

The recuperating intensity of gathering contemplation is more remarkable than ruminating alone, and a few examinations affirm the presence of an expanding influence of harmony in the earth while reflecting in gatherings.

Learning experience improves: this is a specific advantage for fledglings; when you're new to the training, you show up with numerous feelings of dread and questions; however while ruminating in gatherings, you normally do it with individuals that have various degrees of experience. You sit close to somebody who has been doing this for 2 months and somebody who has been doing it for a long time, so you get the opportunity to take in something else from the two points of view.

Input accessibility: you not just get the opportunity to gain from others' encounters, however to get valuable counsel. In the event that you ever get befuddled or need some direction on a specific exercise, your reflection accomplices will be there for you. Nobody is superior to anybody, they all assistance each other through this experience and together, arrive at physical and mental harmony.

Making propensities: a small impediment of contemplating alone at home is the means by which simple you can discover a reason for skipping reflection day. It's much the same as exercise center day or solid eating regimen day; yet when you help to amass reflection, your inspiration gets higher, it urges you to be steady with the training.

Gathering exercises are mentally important: we feel better when doing assemble exercises since we make associations with others, taking advantage of a similar quietness and wellspring of harmony as your contemplation mates can cause you to feel settled, good, upheld and safe.

All things considered, a mental report demonstrated that brainwaves can synchronize while pondering, so the association you feel with your contemplation accomplices isn't just passionate, however physical.

Lessens depression: following these mental realities, feeling desolate is very normal among individuals in our occasions. This is especially intriguing since we have more chances of being associated with others all the time on account of our mobiles and PCs, yet in the event that we can converse with truly anybody at whatever point we need to, why we do we despite everything feel desolate? The appropriate response might be that we don't require advanced associations, however genuine ones, and that is the place share reflection plays it roll.

At the point when we meditate in gatherings, we make a situation of acknowledgment and having a place, we make companions and offer something more than a 'hello' like it ordinarily occurs in our working environments.

EVERYTHING IS BETTER WHEN SHARED—INCLUDING MEDITATION.

Much the same as music, reflection can be appreciated all alone or with other people who move to a similar beat. You can feel a genuine association with others by taking advantage of a similar quiet and wellspring of harmony simultaneously. Truth be told, we can truly meet individuals on a similar frequency: recorded EEG results show that brainwaves synchronize while thinking.

RUMINATING WITH A GROUP HELPS TO DEVELOP A HABIT.

It's anything but difficult to track down reasons not to ruminate at home. Much the same as meeting companions at the exercise center for bunch wellness class can rouse you to work out, finding a reflection gathering can give the vital support to building up a steady practice.

CRITICISM IS AVAILABLE.

Reflection bunches regularly incorporate experts of changing levels. In case you're new to reflection, you may locate that different individuals from your gathering can help clear up any disarray you may have over various sorts of contemplation, assist you with discovering answers tending to troubles with training, and give input in regards to encounters that emerge during the contemplation procedure.

JOINING A GROUP IS ACTUALLY PHYSICALLY GOOD FOR US.

As indicated by the book "Bowling Alone: The Collapse and Revival of American Community" by Robert D. Putnam, joining a gathering can cut your danger of passing on in the following year into equal parts!

Forlornness is presently demonstrated to be terrible for our wellbeing. A situation of acknowledgment and having a place are ideal conditions under which social creatures like us can flourish.

BE A PART OF THE BIGGER PICTURE.

A gathering can all the more likely help a person's internal excursion. It's moving and spurring to interface with other people who share our aims for world harmony. It is simpler to apply Gandhi's recommendation to "be the change you wish to find on the planet" when you are a piece of an aggregate group. As per Andrew Kelley at The Boston Buddha, it is likewise a decent method to "all in all bind together and add solidarity to our aims" with a typical gathering objective regardless of whether the objective is simply to be progressively loose and less responsive.

THERE IS POWER IN NUMBERS.

In all honesty, there are examines that demonstrate the presence of a far reaching influence of harmony in the general condition when a gathering reflects together. As per the brought together field superstring hypothesis in material science, rushes of vibration stream from everything known to mankind influencing the aggregate awareness. Gatherings have the ability to breath life into that field. Cell scientist Bruce Lipton states in his book "Science of Belief" that our awareness can change the physical world around us by modifying the field. A fascinating trial tried a hypothesis called "The Maharishi Effect" in Merseyside, England. A number that surpassed one percent of the populace ruminated together consistently from 1988 to 1991, and the crime percentage dropped so much that Merseyside went from third most elevated to the least positioned city in England during the hour of the investigation. In the interim, the control town of non-meditators held a consistent crime percentage. Reflection was the main factor in the investigation that could represent the change, as the researchers determined that police rehearses, neighborhood financial matters, and socioeconomics continued as before all through the examination.

In all honesty, there are considers that demonstrate the presence of a gradually expanding influence of harmony in the general condition when a gathering reflects together.

As Margaret Mead once stated, "Never question that a little gathering of individuals can change the world. Without a doubt it is the main thing that has."

Reflection classes and gatherings can frequently be found in perfect, agreeable, mainstream conditions like yoga studios or at explicit contemplation associations like Unplug in Los Angeles or Stil Studio in Boston, with a lot all the more opening up in the middle of the two coastlines. In New York City there's The Path, which is a spring up contemplation bunch that changes areas consistently both to keep things new and to demonstrate that we needn't bother with ideal conditions to reflect. Or then again, on the off chance that you can't locate a neighborhood gathering, you could begin your own utilizing the "Get Together" application. As opposed to permitting innovation to turn into an interruption, you can make it work in support of you! You can utilize an application to discover or begin a gathering. Maybe every week somebody could bring a top choice, guided contemplation to impart to the gathering—from an application, yoga site, or YouTube video, for instance. This keeps things new and the expectation to absorb information goes up.

Thinking in a gathering is a fun and solid approach to mingle and gain proficiency with another ability that is useful for our brain, body, and soul. Take contemplation bunch pioneer and creator of "Glad Yoga" Steve Ross' recommendation: "Focus on the inside, take a full breath, and make a plunge!"

Chapter 9: The Art Of Cultivating Stillness And Relaxation

Although we are often unaware of it, we have total relaxation at our disposal in almost every moment of our lives, whatever the circumstances. Our emotions, stress, and the general busyness of our lives typically obscure this choice. If we don't have experience in deliberately accessing a state of relaxation, it can be difficult to remember that even this is an option. Meditation offers an introduction to a relaxation toolkit at every moment. As you become more familiar with using this, it becomes easier to remember that you always have a choice. The meditations in this section aim to help you relax. When you practice them more over time, you may find that you are also using them more often. I trust you do.

Now that you have read and understood how we create and maintain insomnia, you may begin to realize what kind of things you will have to do to start your recovery. If so, then the method already works. But if not, then don't despair. I'm about to give you step-by-step instructions on how to tackle your problem exactly.

JUST MAKE A PROMISE

The Guided Meditation for Sleep and Mindfulness insomnia program consists of 12 promises, 12 commitments, not 12 cast-iron rules. Make these promises part of an honest commitment to getting better, and you become more than a rule-followere—you become responsible for creating yourself a better life. Do not 'obey the rules' since somebody tells you what to do. Make the following promises because you understand the effect they will have on your sleep and because you are committed to returning to normal sleep. It should not be difficult to make those promises. Stick to them with energy, optimism, dedication, and a sense of goodness. Seen in this way, it is not a hardship to follow the program; it is an empowerment. You take control; you take responsibility, you commit to getting over your problem.

Sleep Hygiene – The Six Promises First

The Guided Meditation for Sleep and Mindfulness promises 1 – 6 concern what experts call 'sleep hygiene.' This is a very basic, non-drug solution that is effective in virtually all early insomnia cases. Sleep hygiene is actually just a collection of common-sense behavioral instructions that help restore regular habits of sleeping. Whether you have intermittent insomnia or have never attempted sleep hygiene before, the pace at which such assurances will make a difference can well shock you. They are incredibly powerful, but easy, and enforcing good sleep hygiene at an early stage can almost always stop a problem from being chronic.

If your problem is a recent occurrence or if you're not sure what kind of insomnia you're, you'll still get all the advice in the Effortless Sleep Process. However, it may be best to continue by following just the first six guidelines. For most, to stick to the first six guidelines would be all it takes to start sleeping well again.

The entire plan must be pursued by all of you with a more serious or long-term issue—including the first six commitments. Don't think you can skip six of the first promises and move on to the more interesting bit! If you're a long-term, chronic insomniac, sleep hygiene rules may well be familiar to you. If this is the case, there could be a 'been there, done that, didn't work' at this stage. But, is this genuinely true? I say this because the majority of long-term insomniacs have pursued sleep hygiene laws at some point, but a few sleepless nights here or there have contributed to their abandoning the whole idea. In fact, do you think that your insomnia is just too severe to be helped by something so simple?

The fact is that when it came to curing myself, even after 15 years of chronic insomnia, actually sticking to these guidelines had a huge effect on my sleeping habits. Such guidelines are strong, and how much difference they can make is astounding. Sleep hygiene laws alone may not be sufficient to cure a chronic insomniac, but they lay a very strong framework for sleep-conducing conditions. Those are the perfect conditions to work their magic on the other promises. And don't make it impossible for yourself: follow the instructions for sleep hygiene even if you've done them before, and give the rest of the group a fair chance to win. One thing is certain: if your sleep hygiene remains bad, you will have a very difficult time keeping the other promises.

The first six guidelines for sleep hygiene should be a part of your life. This guideline is designed not only for the occasional or recent sufferer, but for long-term insomniacs in particular. For many, negative beliefs and contributory self-defeating behaviors mean that sleep hygiene alone, though essential, may not be enough to overcome insomnia.

What Is Missing from Conventional Sleep Hygiene? – The Next Set of Six Promises

There are several books that provide solutions to the problems of sleep. Nearly all of these believe insomnia is all about what happens in the night. The fact is, poor sleep patterns sometimes extend beyond the bedroom and into daily life, and if you're a chronic insomniac, the core of your recovery would be to continue to believe you should sleep. The crucial distinction between this and other interventions is that we discuss not only the habits associated with 'going to bed,' but also those directly correlated with and promoting negative thoughts and flawed sleep beliefs. Promises 6 – 12 are more focused on those long-term sufferers who are unlikely to have tried many remedies and techniques. Such assurances are more concerned with shifting your potentially negative attitudes about sleep. The next section will explain how you can see the values shifting unconsciously in attending to negative behaviors, and the problem slipping away. The good thing is that it is fairly straightforward to change such habits.

Preparation-Make Things Easier on Your Own

There are a few common-sense things you can do in preparation before you embark on the program. They are not in themselves 'laws' or rigid instructions, but rather subtle improvements in lifestyle that many people think to make sleep just that little bit easier.

- Cut out stimulants before bed – I'd still hear men, including doctors, after 15 years asking me if I'd try to cut back on my coffee intake. My frustration would sometimes get the better of me, 'No!' I'd say with feigned amazement, I'd never think coffee could keep me going! In the unlikely case that you don't realize that coffee will keep you awake, and if you're drinking multiple cups of coffee a day, or if you're drinking coffee or cola later in the day, be mindful that this could have a negative impact on your pillow. Similarly, if vodka and Red Bull are your favorite tipple, don't be surprised if you find it difficult to sleep after a night out. In the morning, coffee should be reduced to one or two cups.

If you drink more than this, then you have a good chance it will affect your sleep, and don't underestimate the impact of a powerful cup of tea. Limit your intake of tea again, and do not drink it at night. There's even a surprising amount of caffeine in Cola drinks, so view cola-like coffee and stop getting it drunk at night. When it's time to go to bed, if you still feel 'wired,' it could well be that you are very prone to caffeine.

Bear in mind that the sensitivity to caffeine will grow at any point in your life, even if you have not previously found it especially stimulating. Experiment with cutting it down or removing it entirely for a couple of weeks, even though you do not think it affects you. Only then do you know for sure if it has an effect on your sleep? Giving up doesn't need to be forever, and at a later date, you can still go back to drinking coffee and tea if you think removing it doesn't make any difference.

Get some hype! – If you're tired all day but wide awake when it gets to bed, that's often because you didn't have enough exercise. Getting to bed at the end of a long, tiring day is one of the greatest free enjoyments in life. If your muscles are tired, then it can be pretty delicious to get into bed and rest. Sadly, you are more likely these days to spend your working life hunched up all day in front of a computer screen or sitting at a desk. If you're very sedentary throughout the day, then your body will be stressed even though you might be exhausted when you go to bed, so it will take you a lot longer to relax enough to fall asleep. Exercise has a huge impact on mood as well and can be very powerful against depression. If you're too inclined to enter a gym or class, go for a brisk walk or jog, run or use a DVD celebrity's workout. It doesn't matter as long as it makes you feel exhausted physically and a little sweaty. You will target at doing at least three workouts a week. A little every day is easier for insomniacs than a rigorous workout once a week.

Declutter your surroundings – In particular, do what you can in the early days to make your bed and bedroom as comfortable as possible. If your mattress is lumpy and old, then fix it. Purchase some fresh cotton bedding 100 percent. And don't skimp on the duvets and pillows. Buy the highest quality which you can afford. Most people spend more on a jacket or a pair of shoes they wear for a couple of months than they do on bedding, which they use for years every night. When you're not allergic to feathers, the luxury of a feather pillow and duvet is worth it. If you can't afford these items, then ensure that your bedding is still freshly washed. To make the sheets clean and welcoming, buy some fabric conditioner with a good scent or apply some starch to the wash.

It's almost difficult for many people to fall asleep when they're too cold, and many find that simply being warmer in bed will alleviate a winter sleeping problem. Most people sleep best in a cool room, in a warm bed. Either switch off the heating and line up the pillow or use an electric blanket. Wearing socks and placing a second duvet on the bed during winter will make a big difference. If it gets too hot later, you can always kick them out. Once you get into bed, you have to be very warm and relaxed. When your insomnia is serious, then the first few minutes in bed are crucial; when you have to 'warm-up' this time, you have a much poorer chance of quickly falling asleep.

If summer weather makes it impossible to have a cool room, then try a fan. Many people use a fan every night, even in winter, because the 'white noise' it produces is really calming and can be almost hypnotic aside from its cooling qualities. Moreover, most people are the best sleeping in a very dark room. Use some blackout curtains to make sure the rising sun doesn't wake you up before you're ready if the sun rises early where you live. You can experiment with eyeshades as well, but make sure they are loose and very comfortable-with Velcro fastenings. The elasticated ones found on aircraft are usually too tight, and may eventually disturb you.

Chill out – If you're a generally tense or anxious person, then you're going to have a more difficult time than someone who naturally tends to get chilled. Set aside time to relax or meditate, even if it's just 15 minutes a day. You may be amazed at the effect this can have on your overall life, and the more relaxed you become when you get to bed, the greater your chances of sleeping. This isn't the same as the bedtime relaxation methods I speak about later in the book, but instead applies to how comfortable your 'current' state is, the state you are in when you get to bed. It can be extremely helpful to have a hot bath or douche one hour before bed. In addition to the obvious fact that a bath is pleasant and relaxing, research has shown that as the body cools down, sleepiness begins to reach a peak one hour after the bath.

OK, you're ready? The essence of the Guided Meditation for Sleep and Mindfulness is a collection of twelve promises, twelve vows to get your life back. Many of these may sound familiar, but some may be very different from anything that you've experienced before, which will have an amazing effect on your sleep. What you have to do now is keep those promises and look out for the tests!

Chapter 10: Meditation In The Mind

More and more we see countless recommendations to practice the age old art and science of meditation these days. Most, if not all, extol its seemingly magical power on the human psyche through its purported benefits. These recommendations and claims have stood the test of time- they are universally accepted and well justified. For eons past those who came before us have spoken volumes regarding this great gift we all posses but today sometimes, we neglect to use. Why now are we again reminded of this?

All of us are participating either aware or unaware. in a quantum shift bringing at times, tumultuous changes in all areas of our society and world structures. No one is exempt from the effects these rapid changes bring. While universally experienced, these trans-formative energies are individually unique and processed differently depending on a person's outlook. With a little discipline and practice we can apply this gift of meditation to help balance stress levels, reduce mind-movies which seem to play nonstop to bring increasing levels of joy, clarity and purpose into life.

While it's true that meditative practices are known by many names in virtually all cultures each with various forms of practice, finding one that will work for you is quite easy. Best of all, this gently leads us ultimately to a special place we often desire and want- greater understanding and acceptance to life's mysteries.

So, let's briefly explore the subject for the sole purpose of learning how to reap many beneficial rewards available through meditation. Besides, it is true, the best things in life are free. So let us begin to clear our minds of useless, wayward abstract thoughts having no justification to control or dictate our life's direction. We will find meditation allows you in the purest sense, to create your own life's experiences. (More discussion about that possibility a bit later). For now, consider that during meditation you can replace, and clear out unwanted thoughts with life affirming versions gaining- a true, lasting peace of mind, body and soul. Meditation is your gateway offering all that and more...you can even create some magic in your life through this simple process!

As you may have heard or if you are already a dedicated practitioner, individuals report profound psychological, physical and spiritual well-being as they practice meditation daily. What then is meditation really all about? For beginners, how can one start? And how far can I go with sincere dedication? Here we are going to examine a few areas- some historical background, benefits, science of the mind and advanced possibilities.

What is Happening In your Brain During Meditation?

Scientists have only recently developed tools sophisticated enough to see what goes on in your brain when you meditate. Clearly, some profound changes occur within the brain. Our brain appears to interact and be directly influenced by our higher-minds and consciousness itself.

Frontal cortex - is the most highly evolved part of the brain, responsible for reasoning, planning, emotions and self-conscious awareness. During meditation it tends to go offline.

Parietal lobe - processes sensory information about the surrounding world, orienting you in time and space. During meditation, activity in the parietal lobe slows down.

Thalamus - is the gatekeeper for the senses. It focuses your attention by funneling some sensory data deeper into the brain and stops other signals in their tracks. Meditation reduces the flow of incoming information to a trickle.

Reticular Formation - receives incoming stimulus and puts the brain on alert, ready to respond. Meditation dials back the arousal signal.

After training in meditation for eight weeks, subjects show a pronounced change in brain-wave patterns, shifting from the alpha waves of aroused, conscious thought to the theta waves that dominate the brain during periods of deep relaxation. Even people meditating for the first time will register a decrease in beta waves, a sign that the cortex is not processing information as actively as usual. After their first 20-minute session, patients show a marked decrease in beta-wave activity.

Rebirth through Breath

Beyond all the medical community assertions lies a vast segment of the population seeking additional benefits when practicing meditation. How can what appears initially only to be a physical act, effect our true inner being so profoundly by simply clearing our conscious thoughts and focusing on our breath? Well the secret really is in our breath. When you first start a meditative practice at face value, it appears really easy. Yet, early on many are easily frustrated because they have really never truly attempted to quiet their thoughts while awake. Successfully navigating the mental mind field of what apparently appears to be non-stop streams of thoughts popping up can at first be a daunting task. Be forewarned this is a common occurrence and quite normal and there is a solution. It's funny actually once realization sets in that you really are like two individuals within a single physical body. And that is not far from the truth.

I, like many who meditate found out early on one key to successfully get beyond this mental speed bump is to acknowledge the thought. Proceed to then dismiss it entirely or agree to revisit the thought after the meditation session and return the mind's focus to your breathing. I have used this method to great success getting past the egos gate keeper role which it often plays.

You may find this method helpful as well if not, find what brings your focus back without distracting thoughts. Again, breathing's role is of utmost importance in this whole process because it is the gateway bridging the physical body with the spiritual body. The goal here is what I refer to as the death of thoughts through focusing on your breath. Becoming more sensitive of taking no thought along with staying present in the moment by the simple act being consciously aware of your breathing, an amazing inner rebirth begins. Next, we define some good basic steps for all meditation practices.

Meditation Techniques New Meditators Should Know to Help Their Meditation Voyage

Learning to meditate is one of the most important skills you can master and the sooner you learn to meditate the sooner you will gain more control over your life. Meditation in essence is about finding your inner peace but there is more to meditation than just finding your inner peace. You can use meditation to help you in every aspect of your life. There are four core meditation techniques that every new meditator should learn.

These four meditation techniques cover different aspects of your life. For example one of the techniques I will cover include Deep-Breathing Meditation which you use to help you to relax and to prepare your mind for meditation and Affirmation

Meditation allows you to reprogram your mind from being negative to positive.

Whilst this is a simplistic view of these two meditation techniques, it highlights the issue that there are varying meditation techniques you can use to improve your life. Lets look at the four basic meditation techniques all new meditators should learn to help you in your meditation voyage.

Mantra Meditation

Mantra meditation is another simple technique for those who are new to meditation. If keeping your mind completely quiet feels like too much of a challenge, mantra meditation might be easier. It combines some of the benefits of positive affirmations with the benefits of meditation with the repetition of a single word or sound. Some people feel a little uncomfortable with the idea of repeating "om" or humming, but you can use whatever mantra you like. As with walking meditation, the key ingredient with mantra meditation is the meditative state you achieve and not necessarily the mantra you use, though it's a good idea to choose a mantra you're comfortable with. This is an easy one to start with.

Walking Meditation Technique

Walking Meditation involves learning to walk whilst meditating. I can hear it now, how are you going to close your eyes whilst walking. Well whether you realise it or not many monastic communities have regularly used walking meditation interspersed with traditional seated meditation to help break up the long periods of meditation.

The walking meditation works by getting you to first control your breathing using the Deep-Breath Meditation Technique and then to use the White-Light Meditation Technique to help learn to control your mind. Just like I mentioned earlier with the counting technique, if your mind starts to wander whilst walking due to mind chatter, you simply stop the counting process and simply start again.

One of the other aspects you need to consider with this technique is to focus on your body and the connection your body has with its path. For each step during the walking meditation technique, you need to feel the path and each step that you are taking. For example you need to be focusing on the feeling in your feet, your ankles, your legs, your arms and so forth.

The Walking Meditation technique is one of those ones you can practice anywhere and you will probably find that it will take you some period of time to conquer this technique without your mind wandering. Make sure that you do not punish yourself if your mind does wander or start to chatter. Simply acknowledge the wandering and bring the mind gently back into the meditated awareness and continue on your way.

Most people when they first think about meditation simply see it as a way to relax however your mind is an incredibly powerful tool and you can utilize meditation to change many aspects of your behaviour, the way you speak and present yourself and the vast professional meditation practitioners will help you to develop these techniques to improve yourself. These four techniques are the first you will learn as you begin to unleash the power meditation can provide as food for your body, mind and soul.

Chocolate Meditation

When you're looking at how to meditate, here's a relatively quick and savory technique to try. The chocolate meditation is a form of mindfulness meditation that's often used in mindfulness-based stress reduction (MBSR) classes, is simple for beginners, engages several senses, and has a built-in reward of making the taste of chocolate feel more intense. Using dark chocolate for this exercise brings its own benefits. If you're looking for something simple and new, try the chocolate meditation.

Use A Popular Meditation App for A quick Refresher.

There are many great meditation apps to try. I recommend downloading several free apps until you find one that feels like a good fit. When working with clients, the first two I recommend are Insight Timer and Headspace. Headspace is great for beginning technique and Insight Timer has many incredible free guided meditations for a wide range of experiences and expertise.

Deepen Your Experience of Eating During Lunch By Being Mindful.

Instead of rushing through each bite, savor them. Notice the smell of the food, how it looks, and the complexity of its taste. Bring your awareness to what it feels like to chew and swallow. Give yourself permission to be fully present in eating or conversations.

This type of meditation will help you reset and re-focus for the second half of your day.

Step Outside To Try A Refreshing Walking Meditation.

Get outside of the office and deep within yourself. Standing still, bring your awareness to your feet, ankles, calves, knees, hamstrings, quads, and your hips. Begin walking slowly and really notice what it feels like to walk--how many moving parts are involved in each simple step. Synchronize your breath with each step for bonus points.

This type of active meditation is not only relaxing, it can help you release unnecessary tension from your mind and body.

Experiment with Repeating A Silent Mantra.

Feel free to create your own mantra or phrase to repeat during meditation. You can pick something as simple as "relax," or "I am here, I am present, I am ready." After you've decided what mantra you'd like to focus on, start repeating it over and over again in your mind. Align your words with your breath so that it can be rhythmic and consistent.

This type of meditation can help prepare you for upcoming events when you need to perform your best.

Breathing Meditation

Breathing meditation is one of the most popular forms of meditation because of its ease and simplicity, as well as its convenience (breathing is always occurring, so it's a convenient anchor for meditation). The breath provides a natural focus that's unobtrusive, but always there, and creates a natural rhythm to get lost in. You can practice breathing meditation for a few minutes, or for longer, and always find relaxation.

Before Jumping Into Your Task List, Take Five Minutes To Count Your Breaths.

As little as five minutes can make a big difference in your day. One of the easiest ways to engage in mindfulness meditation is to focus on the breath.

Sit comfortably. Close your eyes. Now take natural, even, rhythmic breaths. While you're breathing in, count one, when you breathe out, count two. Once you get up to the count of 10, start over at one.

This simple meditation technique is excellent for beginners and individuals that want to develop razor-sharp focus.

Change It Up With A Visualization-Based Meditation.

For something new, try visualizing something. This can be as simple as imaging yourself sitting by a stream. As you're sitting at this stream, notice how beautiful the clear blue water is as it flows right to left. When you notice a thought, visualize it as a leaf on the stream. Watch it float away as you remain in the calm presence of watching this scene take place.

This type of meditation is great for re-connecting to the present moment. Sometimes there are many leaves--and that's perfectly okay! Notice them and you are meditating.

That's what's amazing about meditation--there are millions of ways to practice, and not a single one of them is wrong.

Hit the pause button at work. Reconnect to your breath. And feel the deep peace that is always accessible when coming into contact with the present moment.

Mini-Meditations

For those who feel they don't have time for full-length meditation sessions (20 minutes is a good average amount of time), or for those who would like to experience some of the benefits of meditation between longer sessions, mini-meditations (meditations around 5 minutes in length) are a great technique to try. Mini-meditations are very simple and fit in well with even the busiest of schedules. Learn how to meditate in shorter bursts, and work up to longer sessions, or just use this technique for quick and convenient stress relief.

White-Light Meditation Techniques

The White-Light meditation technique is an extension of the Deep-Breath Meditation Technique in that you will use Deep-Breath Meditation to get control of your mind and body and then step into a second stage where you will use objects in your minds eye to maintain control of your brain chatter.

Buddhist Monks have been know to teach their young monks this technique by getting them to focus on counting however you can use any object to help you gain and maintain focus. Essentially what this technique does is to get the meditator to start by focusing on the number one as they breathe in. Then in your minds eye you then focus on the next number, which is the number 2 and maintain that focus as you breathe out and then breathe in again. You then change the number to number 3 as you breathe out and in again. You continue counting through the number system until you loose control and focus. For example, if for one moment you think about the dinner you are going to have, then you must start from the number one again.

You keep following this process during each meditation session. Once you have mastered this technique you will find it is easier to get focus during a meditation session as you will not allow your mind to wander.

Bath Meditation

One soothing method for those looking at how to meditate is the bath meditation. A bath meditation combines the standard benefits of meditation with the benefits of a soothing, hot bath, which can relax tired muscles, provide a relaxing atmosphere, and allow a temporary feeling of escape from stressors. Being in the water can also help you to stay awake, something that is important but sometimes challenging if you're learning how to meditate when tired. Try a bath meditation, and be clean, relaxed, and ready for bed (or a low-stress day) when you're finished.

This technique is great for relaxing and feeling grounded.

Affirmation Meditation Techniques

Affirmation Meditation is a technique that allows the meditator to slowly train their own subconscious to follow a different attitude. For example, how many times a day to you say negative things like "That will never work" or "I will never get that job."

When you are in a state of calm and focus gained by using the Deep-Breath Meditation Technique and White-Light Meditation technique your subconscious can be more easily manipulated to change those inbuilt negative attitudes. Whilst you can certainly change your attitude and response to situations using your conscious mind, quite often you will find that little things will penetrate through.

The objective of the Affirmation Meditation Technique is to slowly reprogram your subconscious so that you can overcome those negative attitudes with more appropriate responses. Like all meditation techniques, this can sometimes take a long period to conquer but is certainly worthwhile.

Deep-Breathing Meditation Techniques

Deep-Breath Meditation is the first technique that all new meditators will be shown. This meditation technique involves learning how to breathe and to control your breath during meditation. This technique is sometimes called the Stillness meditation technique.

Learning to use the Deep-Breath Meditation technique will teach you how to control your heart rate, your breathing and also your ability to maintain control over your mind. All of us suffer from brain-chatter where we talk to ourselves. Apart from just controlling our breathing, we start off using this technique to get control of our mind and body. Once you have mastered this technique it allows you then to use other Meditation Techniques to improve yourself. Other meditation techniques you can use are the affirmative meditation technique and walking meditation technique.

The other key advantage of mastering the deep-breathing meditation technique is that once you understand how to breath effectively using deep breaths to get control of your stress and emotions, you can use the techniques outside of meditation to quickly get control in a stressful situation. The more you practice the deep-breath meditation technique the better you will get at it.

Chapter 11: Bring Life And Meditation Together

Figure 8: Free Credits

As it has been emphasized in this book, meditation is a way of transforming yourself, and this should occur through dedication and training yourself to follow the right attitudes and actions. If you do not maintain your discipline during this process, then you will be wasting your time. The changes you will see in your life will be minimal. For you to see significant changes, you must maintain your concentration and have the discipline to ensure that you are determined to achieve your goals. It requires that you observe determination, vigilance, and perseverance and be sincere to yourself. Through this way, you will ensure that the changes that are happening to your over the period that you keep practicing are real, and they will last. When you train your mind, it will be possible to live following a particular way of life even as we do our daily activities.

Remember, in modern society, we are faced with a lot of hustles, and this could make use face anxiety. It is through the meditation exercises that we can do away with this. We can use it to cultivate a life whereby we are happy. We can live it to the fullest since we know how we can deal with the hurdles that we meet on our daily activities.

The kind of life we face today is the reason we find that we get faced with a lot of worries. It is because there are things that affect our lives that we may not be able to achieve even when they are essential to us. Dedicating some time, even if we do it for about 30 minutes, to meditate is essential. It will enable us to become better. The impact is that it gives our day a completely new look. Doing this will change the way you view things from a negative to positive thinking. It will also change the way you approach things as well as how you relate with people within your environment. You will find strength so that even when you experience tough stuff in your day, you will be able to handle them in the right way possible. You will also move on to other things whereby you will perform well. The good thing with meditation is that its effects remain in your mind. As you continue doing it, you find that you are becoming a better and better person since its effects are cumulative.

When you do this over and over, it will stick to your brain, and with time, you will be doing it with ease.It is something you will get used to with time, and you will continue to experience these benefits for the longest time possible. Be familiar with the meditation exercises because you must keep experiencing these benefits.

It is only fair to say that you have a lot of things to do. So how will you handle your family and professional life? The best part with meditation is that whether you are a committed professional or you are busy with your family life, you can always find the right time. Discover when you can do it because it is compatible with these kinds of experiences. You are the person who is controlling your life, and as such, you know when to create the time to perform meditation exercises. Through it, you will be able to see the more excellent picture of your life. If you have been facing your life with uncertainty, it is high time you eliminate this. It is possible by starting meditation. You will start seeing your life in the right direction. You need altruism and confidence and meditation happens to be the best way to do this.

Chapter 12: Self-Healing Process

Self-healing refers to the process of recovering from psychological or mental disturbances and trauma. The process is directed and motivated by the patient concerned and guided by instinct. Self-motivation plays a vital role in the self-healing process. Everyone should be able to control their emotions and how they react to different things. As we focus on self-healing, we understand that we are in full control of ourselves. The mind is allowed to concentrate, think, and direct emotions. It can be guided by a professional or done by the individual by following the required guideline. Meditation helps in the reflection of past events and allows the mind to think about current events and design future coping mechanisms. Self-healing does not happen overnight, but it is a continuous process that can bring fruitful results when practicing as expected. It has always been said that time can heal a broken heart. Psychologists, however, have discovered that words too can heal. Use the right words and do not associate with people who always say negative words to you and bring you down.

Before beginning the self-healing process, know and understand the things that agitate you and your stressors. Constant encounters with those can significantly slow down the healing process. Psychological mechanisms often improve the physical and mental conditions of a person. Some of the mechanisms include breathing, meditation, imagery, yoga, and fitness exercises. Emotions have a direct impact on our bodies. The inner feelings are usually a reflection of what we see outside. Anxiety can hurt our lives. Meditation during agitation ensures that stress is released from the mind and the body. This is because, during meditation, the mind relaxers, and the body calms. As this process occurs, stress will be released from the mind that's helping reduce anxiety. Studies have shown that consistent practice of meditation can help cure anxiety and any other mental health problems. Short-term meditation process can help prevent depression and anxiety. This is because the mind will always be relaxed and able to handle the various stressors. Because of day-to-day life struggles, we still find ourselves caught up in some situations that can make us anxious.

In most cases, meditation concerns with inner healing. We want to be happy and come but dealing with bad bosses at work, traffic jams that can delay us on the road, and expecting something that we are not sure if we will get. These are some of the situations that can make us nervous during the self-healing process. We can concentrate on breathing exercises and some meditation techniques when faced with things that make us and shares; we need to focus on achieving a healthy and peaceful mind. As you practice meditation, so does the self-healing process take place.

Observe the following steps during self-healing:

☐ Set time for meditation. For instance,

you can set aside 15 minutes for meditation alone. During that time, your mind wanders as the body relaxes. Meditation should be your daily routine, just like the things you do each morning like preparing breakfast, brushing teeth, and taking a shower. Fifteen minutes of meditation in the morning can work wonders, and if you are consistent, you will realize tremendous results. During lunch, you can try to meditate for as little as 10 minutes. This second meditation exercise will give you the energy to finish the rest of the day. This can also provide you with time to reflect on how things are going and appreciate yourself for being the best you can. Saying you are busy is just an excuse and should not be used as a reason not to practice meditation.

☐ Involve friends during meditation. Sometimes when we are anxious or doubled, we share our problems with our friends and those close to us. By doing this, it helps us to be relieved and feel good with ourselves. As we share our troubles with our friends, we need to meditate as well. Invite your friend so that you can do the meditation together. As you do this together, you will release yourself from anything that is challenging you. You can choose a place that the two of you find comfortable and free to meditate. You can also put the guided meditation on speakerphone so that both of you can understand it together. It has always been the same that sharing is caring, so the need for cohesiveness and unity.

☐Do not be restricted. I understand that meditation can be done anywhere at any time. You can have your schedule depending on availability. Be in charge of the routines you have set. Understand that you are doing this for your good and betterment of your health.Know the risks of anxiety and appreciate the health benefit of meditation for anxiety. Do not be preoccupied with other stuff that you feel are more important.Treat meditation as very important, as well. Lack of restriction gives you free will to choose and reschedule if things do not go on as you planned.

When we are silent as we meditate, our nervous system is reorganized, and our body can experience natural healing. You need to accept in your mind that meditation is a healing exercise and an excellent remedy for anxiety. Many people have been using meditation as the most natural healing for anxiety. If well conducted, it may prevent someone from taking antidepressants. Some people have raised concerns that no matter how much they try to be still, it is not easy to feel the quietness. However, this is true in most circumstances, especially if there are so many things disturbing someone. The things that concern your mind during this process are very healthy. The chaotic thought usually happens immediately; you start the meditation process. It is straightforward to try and push the thoughts away so that you can concentrate. You need to realize that the thoughts are as a result of your mind designing a way of coping and healing itself. Allow the thoughts and feelings to come through then continue your breathing exercises. Let thoughts linger naturally in your mind. Allow them to occupy your mind, and as you go on, you will realize that slowly, your mind will be free.

The self-healing process begins in mind as people fill their minds with positive thoughts and attributes. They become relaxed, active, and the heart best also slows down. During this process, it is important to appreciate yourself and forgive yourself for reacting the way you did. Blaming oneself for being responsive over their anxiety only worsens the situation and slows down the healing process. Anxiety, when not treated, can lead to adverse brain effects. It is not healthy for the mind and body. People who are more anxious are more susceptible to depression, insomnia, high blood pressure, and madness. There is no one known cause of anxiety, but emotional triggers vary from one person to the other. Meditation, therefore, comes in handy and gives you various techniques com how to handle your stressors before they get hold of you. Create a peaceful environment that is serene and comfortable. You can also draft encouraging words on the wall where you can see, and as you meditate, think about how those words encourage and motivate you. Be in control of your environment and let the people you stay with, if any, know your sessions to avoid interruptions. Distractions slow down the meditation since the mind will not be at ease. It will also mean that the mind is not settled, and a serious soul search cannot happen. Treat meditation for anxiety exercises just like you would do for medicine prescribed. If you have to reschedule, make sure you do it when that time reaches. Do not procrastinate since procrastination is like defaulting medication. Procrastination is also a severe threat to meditation exercise and can prevent full healing; it may also make the problem worse.

Healing is a process, so the need to be patient and surround yourself with positive people. While some people experience self-healing a lot faster, others take time. This is because we experience anxiety on different levels, and what triggers anxiety on someone may not trigger anxiety on the other. If you do not feel healed for the duration set, feel free to contact a professional. I'm this situation; mindful meditation for anxiety can be done with the guidance of a professional. Also, if you cannot focus on your own, consider joining a class near you. You can also adopt some useful relaxation techniques to help your mind calm. Self-healing has also been used as a remedy for other mental related issues. This means that besides being a remedy for anxiety, you will also enjoy additional benefits like having a peace of mind. Self-healing also helps you accept yourself for who you are and be your motivator towards your success. Self-healing has been very proven and can be quickly done by anyone. Identify a safe person you can tell your problems. A reliable person can be that friend who does not judge you and always have calming words. They have your best interest and correct you with love. They also assure you that no matter what happens, they got your back.

Complete Health Meditation

The scientific community shows that what used to be irrelevant to religion versus traditional medicine is and always has related to your wellbeing. Newtonian theory is outdated because of new findings about the workings of the universe. And, while pharmaceutical and medical populations are aware of the root causes of disease and disease, not many are willing to make those changes because many people in their communities are obviously not only disadvantaged in the administration of health, they are also unemployed. Soon, medicines other than pain medications are mostly obsolete that help to reduce the discomfort of acute symptoms before they are healed. Knowledge is the capacity and ability to detect and correct the root causes of infection and disease in this situation.

Because all drugs are made synthetically, while their relative herbal compounds are generally safe and effective, many of the essential elements such as vitamins and minerals, which can be one of the main reasons they produce adverse or even death-threatening effects, remain outside these medicines. It is medically proven that prescription medicines, combined with traditional medical practices, cause more deaths worldwide than cancer and cardiovascular disease combined and yet the FDA only authorizes its use prior to testing. While pharmaceutical companies have managed to produce safe drugs with no side effects, these medications merely cover up the disease and disease symptoms and put the patient in a painless condition.

People in power appear not to give it up very easily until they have been forced to do so through new legislation that will help us to be secure. Energy companies that do not concern the health and welfare of the people of the world have shown these things time and time again, but rather how much money and control they are. One could infer that worldwide, the number I goal is to eliminate and replace harmful and even lethal practices by totally safe and efficient methods, purely because of the implications that governments want us to think can have for our health and safety.

Everything you really need to learn about the root causes of disease and disease are related to heat, because it's all important. Therefore, if everything consists of energy, it is reasonable to assume that disease and illness are energy sources, or at least energy vibration. A vibration or resonance differentiates what this energy reflects and determines the waves ' potential. Vibration is a frequency, which is called hertz (HZ), in the same way as the music notes. Colors have the same function, since each frequency or vibration is different. Life itself, therefore, is energy, as are our minds, feelings, beliefs and desires.

Every organ and component, including our cells, is fuel, because our bodies are made of energy. Our cells do the work that makes our bodies function properly. To do this, oxygen and water must be present. Each cell is a self-living entity that can perform miraculous procedures and save event memories through our 5 senses. Our bodies are very complex, yet easy to operate.

As with all we do, our cells respond every day to stimuli and store these events as pictures. Our cells continue to operate normally, but when we feel we are at risk from our insecurities, anxiety, worry, doubt or concern, our cells respond to defense by blocking what they need to operate effectively. Whenever a perceived negative state occurs, our cells stop and their energy changes as it happens. Positive environments produce positive energy and negative energy. Positive energy occurs at a higher frequency, which is easily understood and seen.

Almost every negative thing we see is self-induced, and we know that from a very young age. Most of us were told that we were weak or that our intentions were incorrect by someone we felt was wise or someone with whom we trusted. Most of the people I know hear or look at the daily news, generally with bad stuff around us. Most of these negative events turn our worldview in very bad ways, so that we dislike someone we don't meet or care about next. We also start to doubt the things we once believed. This is what is happening in today's country based on the reality of so-called "experts to whom we should listen." Another important aspect of power is the capacity for responsibility for what we've generated so far. Therefore, we are fully responsible for everything we have made. To deny this is a lie that creates more detrimental energy and adds to what we already have. We are on the right track by acknowledging and accepting responsibility and can even begin to see positive change.

Most natural cure treatments specifically address the energy balance in the body to achieve optimal health. Energy curing, like Reiki, has become a real and viable way of treating diseases and diseases that can not even be tackled in traditional techniques. These energy healing techniques target areas that vibrate less often than the rest of the healthy body and increase their vibration to a normal level to return them to full health. A professional energy practitioner can cure many problems that conventional therapies can not, and you will also find that these alternative methods are combined with traditional methods.

When determining the vibratory frequency of healthy cells, we should then be able to develop new technologies capable of producing energy at the same frequency and which could produce results which are like self-healing methods. Imagine going into a power chamber or lying in a computer to increase the intensity of unhealthy cells to a normal healthy level of your vibration. This will become the standard healing method for the future and hopefully in the very near future. The prescription and uncomfortable, timely and costly traditional treatments will virtually be eliminated. Although the energy of the body for the energy healer can be balanced in up to three sessions, a new energy induction technology can achieve the same results in only one session.

Often there is strong resistance to their adoption if revolutionary ideas arise, especially those which would eliminate most of the population in the present industry and that would definitely occur in our present medical and pharmaceutical community. But this new technology is about to be discovered just around the corner. This new technology must be developed to ensure the general health and wellbeing of the world's population so that we can reduce the increasing cost of our current medical procedures and ensure that those with severe and weak diseases and diseases will have longer life.

The more people are aware of this new technology, the more they are motivated to develop new and far improved treatments, to stay healthy, without having to endure the absolvent and often cruel everyday treatment methods.

If financial experts did not predict that the economy would crash, I truthfully assume, that everybody would still do business as usual. Your convictions Each one of us has the right, regardless of its source, to believe or to disbelieve what we hear. The culture is in the wrong direction, because people have very little self-confidence and rely instead on what external sources tell. If you don't listen to them, you can't react negatively. The negative reaction causes the cells to shut down and turn into negative rather than positive vibrations. All it takes is your intuition that something is negative, although it is not necessarily negative. You actively track your well-being based on your beliefs, which actually set the boundaries of your expectations.

Your energy vibration not only produces positive or negative effects in your life. You can obtain and attract depending on what type of energy you produce and intend. If you are afraid of it all, you create a terrible reality that defends your cells and gives you negative energy which will make you sick both physically and emotionally. It is the negative energy that causes disease and disease in your body and particularly in cells, and no medication will heal them before you feel invincible. You won't need these drugs when you get there. Even if you can treat a serious condition, the same infection will likely occur again in the future until the root cause has been solved and fixed. It is mainly because of the stress that we feel and react negatively to, which prevents our cellular memory from stress-inducing events, that cancer and cardiac disease kills so devastating. Until the pressure is removed, the infection or disease may return.

You have powerful knowledge to draw on the root cause of disease, by realizing that the negative energy in our cells is the root cause of disease. However, even with this new understanding, you can still ask the question how you adapt your responses to your situations that decide what your expectations are, because your understanding of your truth gives rise to a positive or negative conviction.

Nevertheless, it should be quite clear at this level that you need to eliminate negativity from your thoughts and beliefs, which undoubtedly is a positive point of departure; but it can be said more easily.

Although this may be a good starting point, it takes years for you to take advantage of the process of creating only positive energy by removing negative ones and transforming them into positive ones, especially because you have a lot to change now, of course. You will not really notice much of the benefits of this change at the beginning of the process, as all your newly created positive energy works to dissolve the total negative energy that you have created throughout your lifetime. It is only when the bulk of this accumulation of negative energy has vanished that you start to see a real positive change happening in your life and.

As I mentioned at the start of this chapter, your suggestions can be used much quicker and easier for meditation than you can imagine. The process is simple and easy when you understand it.

Improvements will take place more easily if you practice your daily meditation, but it will not be a cure for the night. If you want to switch from bad to positive, it can be a real and viable solution.

Then find a quiet and relatively free spot for distractions. If you keep your spine straight, you can sit, lie, or lie on your back. Place your hands on each other's palms, spread your fingers apart and softly touch the tips of your thumbs and toes, as if you had a power ball. Close your eyes and concentrate on the space between your eyes, your Third Eye. Your Third Eye is a link to your spiritual realm.

Start by taking a deep, regulated inhalation through your nose until your lungs are filled with air and pause for some time, then breathe out through the mouth and clear your lungs and stop again before you begin the next breathing cycle. Repeat this breathing pattern as often as you like, before you make statements. Continue the guided breathing pattern during the entire meditation session.

Make connections to your Self by asking, "Can I be connected with my Self." Be mindful that this is not a question, but a suggestion. This is not a question. The words shall I be' such as' I may be' form a permission statement, except when the words are somewhat transposed. Replace this statement with a grateful statement by saying "thank you." Repeat the thank you statement 3 times so that when the second part of your session starts, you are certain that you are fully connected.

So start with your meditation statements and gratefully follow everyone. You should strive to synchronize your statements to an external framework. In general, make a request or command statement while inhaling and then make a thank you statement while you are exhaling. It helps specify and keep a speed for your session.

If you are new to meditation, begin with a request or two, follow each with gratitude. Seek to use the power of 3, each with its corresponding declaration of gratitude and make the second three times, each with its related declaration of gratitude. Repeat as often as possible this sequence. If the session is more convenient, add additional requests using the same template.

Meditation tips for a healthy body and mind

At the outset, meditation was used to open spiritual development to the saint and to the saint's guiding presence. Today, however, meditation is a valuable tool even for those who do not consider themselves religious. It can be a source of peace and silence in a world which is seriously lacking both.

It can be used to cure, purify, balance emotions, deepen the focus, unlock creativity and find guidance within.

Before you start meditation, set your standards apart and don't press the right way to do so. There are many ways to meditate and there are no requirements for proper meditation. Which works is the right way for you. And some experiments and changes may be necessary to find out what works. There are several approaches I have listed below.

But there are things to avoid when you start meditation: do not try to force anything to happen.

Don't overanalyze meditation Don't try to empty your mind or pursue your thoughts. There's no one "right" to meditate. Only focus on the system and find the best way! Choose a time and place to start meditation you won't be interrupted. It could seem like an overwhelming task itself. Without being a hermit, people in your life probably demand your time and attention. You can tell them you'll find your shoes, get your gum out of your head, listen to rants about people at work, or just after a few minutes you've been calm and quiet. Know that you must do it for yourself, but also because you will be more relaxed, energized and loveable.

Only 10 or 15 minutes are needed for your meditation session when you start. It's a lot of time to get going, and you may still feel that you can get away from your busy schedule. That's OK—it's much better to spend a couple of minutes meditating than to put it off absolutely.

Over time, relaxation time can be so effective that you spend more time in a meditative state. That's entirely up to you. A successful intention is to work up to two 20 minutes of meditation every day. Evidence has shown that meditating this time will improve health and reduce stress and pressure every day.

The cycle is improved if you meditate on every day at the same time. Most people find that first in the morning meditation works for them. Some people meditate last night before going to sleep. For everybody, there's no precise time. All that works is good for you! Just make sure you regularly practice.

The real place to meditate is again up to you. Many people put a space in their relaxation room aside, but it's probably too drastic if you start out. You should intend to meditate in your bedroom, in the office, in the kitchen or in the backyard, regardless of where you are concerned. It's easier of course if you don't want to meditate when the other family in the living room watches TV.

Besides that, where you meditate doesn't matter–it's much more important to start practicing meditation.

Don't be afraid to change it once you notice that you haven't worked for the original place. The same applies to your chosen time and method. The total value of meditation goes far beyond the precise method of meditation.

One of the best ways to start meditation is through guided meditation. This is a CD or MP3 with all the instructions you need for a meditation status. You just must find something that will not interrupt you, sit down and play the audio file. Soundstrue.com has a lot of guided pictures and meditation.

There are several different types of meditation. We will cover some of the most popular types below, but if none of them suits you, there will be more to explore on the Internet. Feel free to try some of these meditations before you find one that works well for you.

Centering is motion therapy. There is always a quiet and peaceful place inside you. This position is often called your "calm zone" where you want to live, in the middle of everyday life, in your peaceful center. This focuses on ensuring that your inner light will not be filled by tension and negative thoughts and emotions.

You are rooted in a state of relaxation, concentration, peace and harmony. When you don't concentrate, you are vague, distracted, nervous, and unbalanced.

Successful centering requires minimal effort so that you can focus on the job such as washing, plying and gardening. Be mindful, however, that your family may be more likely to disturb if you see something. Only tell them that you meditate, and they should leave you alone for several minutes if they don't want your food, water, or plant to be inspired. Here are a couple of quick centering techniques. Clear Breath Perception includes you in whatever you do, giving your respiration a few moments... You don't have to be fully focused... Just enough to bring you back to the heart of your calm. Breathe naturally, or maybe slowly and deeper.

Take several deep, slow breaths when you are stressed and dispersed. Only imagine with every breath that you take back to your inner self all your scattered energy and attention... Your relaxed nucleus.

Letting go This centering technique combines breath consciousness with "Let go." Especially useful in stressful situations or negative thinking or feeling. Say,' Let' as you inhale. Say (silently or aloud). Just say "go" as you exhale... Just as you let go of all that stresses you.

Relaxation Meditation This extremely simple and relaxing meditation uses a little-known secret eye. In a soft downward look, the eyes can rest with an immediate automatic calming effect.

Relaxation meditation provides substantially less tension and can be used almost everywhere (but not when driving) for a fast2-minute calming break. You will also become more conscious.

Sit back comfortably upright.

Allow your eyes to rest, look smoothly, but don't concentrate.

Allow your eyes to descend to an elegant level without closing your eyes.

Keep looking down... Your focus is the gazing act (instead of the area you are looking at). You may note a rhythmic respiration.

It's okay to let your attention drift a bit. Let them close if your eyes get very heavy. It's all right. It's all right.

If you are conscious of your comfortable environment, simply bring back to your attention the calm, downward look.

Breathing Meditation In this meditation, you should focus on your breath. It is perhaps one of the best relaxation techniques to begin with.

Start with a comfortable position. Sit comfortably and quite straight with your back as you rest to meditate. It allows the spiritual energy to flow freely into the brain, a key aspect of meditation. Leaning on a chair's back, wall, headboard, etc., is all right. If for medical reasons you can't sit up, lie flat on your back. Place your hands in any comfortable place.

Close your eyes as soon as you relax.

Start noticing your intake. We breathe so often that we naturally take oxygen. Take the time to see your breath.

Remember the oxygen that fills the lungs.

And you remember breathing and leaving the room for the lungs. Repeat the breathing notice process.

As you do, you will notice ideas coming up. It could be about parents, friends, jobs or whatever. This does not matter; it is all part of the process and it is perfectly normal to continue thinking during meditation.

But when these ideas come up, allow your next breath to drift away. Bring your mind every time your thoughts drift back to your breathing.

Walking meditation If you find it difficult to sit still and keep your eyes closed during meditation, it may be good to walk meditation.

There are four components for walking meditation: be aware of your breathing, be aware of your environment and be aware of the movement of your body. Take time to think about your experience in meditation. Know how much you would breathe during your respiratory meditation. Note each breath while encouraging and breathing again.

Be mindful of the air your lungs fill and use every breath to submit intrusive thoughts.

Once you start to notice the climate, you may be surprised. We take many things for granted throughout our lives, and much of what lies around us is unnoticed. When you walk around, you notice the different colors.

Don't just note colors. Look for sounds. Listen for sounds. Look for sounds. Listen for sounds. There can be bird songs, on the road noise or people's conversation or animal talk. Adjust consciously to these different sounds. Notice the numerous songs that the birds sang.

Be careful of the various traffic sounds if you are in an urban area. Each car's engine sounds slightly different. The tones on the different street surfaces are the same. You'll find yourself listening to things that happened just before you.

Smells are also available to fill the senses. Perhaps the freshly mown grass or sweet smell immediately following a rain shower. The air has many tastes, and most of them have passed through your consciousness.

Tune into your skin's movement. Start to notice the light pressure on the soil of your feet as you walk. Whether it is a calm day or a windy day, you know the air that blows your hair. Be mindful about your body's movement as you walk around. Feel like the movement of your arms. Remember how flat, upright or different you hold your head? Take care when you stroll, and you're intrigued by what you see.

Once you walk, take some time to go back to your normal world. During this time, during your meditation you can mentally experience your thoughts and feelings. Imagine what you can do next time you decide to walk to improve your experience.

Return slowly from your peaceful place to your regular world.

This practice comes from an old Indian book, the Malini Vijaya Tantra, which was written about 5000 years ago. The meditation is very simple, but very strong, and can quiet your mind and link you to your essence or Inner Spirit.

This meditation uses a mantra as its focus. A mantra is a word or phrase that can catalyze a transition into a more positive, peaceful state of consciousness. The most famous mantra in this tradition is: Aum. Aum has no language literally. Rather, it is the underlying vibration of the universe. To harmonize with the real sound of the world was the eternal tone of Aummm.

While sometimes this mantra is sung aloud, in this meditation you will mentally repeat the mantra... Silently. Silently. Silently. Silently.

There are some important points before we get to the real steps: one of the keys to this practice is to repeat the mantra slowly or softly.

The benefit of this technique is that you encourage the mind to travel into the deeper realms of consciousness.

Therefore, though focusing on the mantra, it is not the intention of this meditation to concentrate on the mantra.

It discourages you from moving into the deeper realms to work hard to keep your attention focused. Instead, you repeat the mantra with "minimal effort" and give your mind a little space to wander.

Resist the temptation to do something and allow the refrain to do the job.

Such relaxation contributes naturally to a deeper and comfortable state of consciousness. This increases energy transfer into the brain and filters out various physical and emotional toxins. (The degree of detoxification can vary from session to session.) This first starting exercise is better performed at 10 to 15 minutes a day due to this detoxification. After a month or so, it can be up to 20 minutes, but without a few years ' experience, that should be the limit for anyone. It is also recommended that you drink plenty of pure water.

Eventually, when you reach a calm and self-consciousness state, mantra therapy accelerates spiritual development.

Sit comfortably and your eyes are relatively straight, and your neck is closed.

Continue to repeat the mantra in your mind gently.

Repeat the mantra as normal as possible. It's not important to match your breathing with the mantra, but it's good if that happens naturally. Let the mantra appear weaker. Repeat with minimal effort.

Keep repeating the mantra tenderly and permit anything to happen.

If you feel like slipping any time into a sleepy or dreamy state, let it happen.

When you find that your mind has turned the slogan off completely, repeat it softly and continue with little effort.

After 10 or 15 minutes, stop repeating the mantra and slowly get out of your meditation.

Then take time to enjoy the floating and soothing sensation surrounding you after every meditation technique. Breathe deeply, (figuratively) gird your loins with new energy and a deep sense of peace.

Conclusion

I'd like to thank you and congratulate you for transiting my lines from start to finish.

In conclusion, anyone and everyone can practice meditation. More and more evidence keeps piling up. as more and more schools of thought are becoming curious about this process called meditation.

It now begs the question, is meditation's roots based on spirituality? In many ways yes, the yogis are tied to the Hindu religion, the Buddhists to the karmic view and of course the mystic quality of meditation overall.

The belief that we human beings for some ancient reason may have the power to heal ourselves has never been more realistic until recently due to the advent of recent studies, where the proof is becoming more and more concrete.

One of the most obvious benefits of meditation and probably the most important, is the natural development of goodwill to others. Almost always any goal or successful outcome of meditation has been coupled with the undeniable truth that the practitioner becomes a better human being, becomes more compassionate, is wiser, more patient and loving. There has never been anything negative associated with a successful practitioner of meditation.

This is probably because this process doesn't create its reality, but instead it works within the laws of reality. Whatever changes it creates is almost always in accordance to the applicable laws of the universe, mystic or otherwise. If you become a successful practitioner, the description about you would almost always come with a standard bunch of desirable outcomes like enlightened, wisdom, masterful and charisma.

 Additionally, one other obvious quality of meditation is compassion.

As you become more adept at this practice of transcending yourself, your capacity for compassion expands and it ultimately matures. Since with all the positive traits that you acquire while developing as a practitioner, you then become grateful and happy. This character of gratitude pushes out other traits of lesser virtue like resentment, anger and envy. Meditation allows the positive traits to grow and become stronger, so much that it overcomes anything that is negative from the other end of the spectrum.

But yes, we are only human, and we still live in an imperfect world, so no one can expect any perfect system for the meditative arts. Then I guess it all boils down to what works for you. How deep you are willing to get into the life? And what is your desired outcome? If you are able to answer those three questions before you engage in any kind of meditative practice, you are likely going to be successful and satisfied with the results. Coupled with an experienced teacher or even better a certified one, your chance for success is very high.

On the other hand, if you go into this practice and your intent and expectations are not clear and defined.You might be disappointed or become disillusioned since probably you thought you might get some superpowers out of it. True enough we might be dealing with the supernatural here, but it doesn't mean that it is something that will manifest itself at your whim just because you believe in it.

Before you begin practicing meditation please take a good look at your heart and see if your reasons are anchored on humility and the true desire of improving yourself. Other than that, there is the danger of exposing yourself to being deluded into thinking that you have become a higher class of citizen looking down at the rest of us.

Nevertheless, meditation is now at the forefront of becoming the no frills, no fuss totally organic way of healthy emotional, physical, and spiritual living. You cannot go wrong with having the correct meditative lifestyle, you can only become better.

www.ingramcontent.com/pod-product-compliance
Lightning Source LLC
Chambersburg PA
CBHW070100120526
44589CB00033B/947